Lucien Herr

Lucien Herr

Socialist Librarian of the French Third Republic

Anne-Cécile Grandmougin

Translated by *Tegan Raleigh*

Litwin Books
Sacramento, CA

This is a translation of Anne-Cécile Grandmougin's,
Lucien Herr bibliothécaire [Lucien Herr, librarian],
published by enssib as her *Mémoire d'étude* in January 2011.

Copyright 2020

Published by Litwin Books in 2020.

Litwin Books
PO Box 188784
Sacramento, CA 95818

http://litwinbooks.com/

This book is printed on acid-free paper.

CIP data pending.

Table of Contents

General Introduction

Judith Crews

Lucien Herr, librarian—and defender of human rights— for the 21st century

Scarcely known in the English-speaking world, Lucien Herr (1864–1926) served as the librarian at France's most prestigious teacher training college, the École Normale Supérieure[1] in the rue d'Ulm in Paris from 1888 until his death in 1926. Generations of "Normaliens", as the graduates of the school are familiarly called, know about Herr and his incredible erudition, his passion for sharing knowledge with others, and his Socratic methods in encouraging the research projects of the students who passed through the library and checked out the books. They know of his frank outspokenness and deeply rooted convictions that a democratic society should be achieved through rationalism, intellectualism, and science, as opposed to the mysticism, sentimentalism, and religiosity that permeated a large segment of French intellectual life during the 19th century, not only among the bourgeoisie of the Third Republic (1879–1940) but also within the university itself. Moreover, truly "superior" education would be the meeting of minds in analytical and critical thinking, rising largely above the parroted reproduction

---

1 Hereafter abbreviated as "ENS".

of established and unquestioned "truths" that characterized the French university throughout the 19th century, and would promote open access to knowledge and learning—through libraries. Some French people also know that Lucien Herr was one of the pioneers of French socialism, and that he influenced the political thinking of important political leaders (Jaurès, Blum, Péguy), and that his political position was grounded both in his vast erudition in philosophy and science and in his active commitment to the international working class in Europe. Finally, his name will always remain associated with one of the defining socio-political crises that divided French society in the late 19th century, the Dreyfus Affair, as his early conviction of the innocence of Dreyfus was behind the galvanization of the French intellectuals who would be known as the Dreyfusards.

Today, 93 years after his death, Lucien Herr has become more relevant than ever. He was a political refugee forced to leave his birthplace during his 9th year; an intrepid and curious traveler during the 1880s who would learn Russian—completely on his own, and during the same year he was preparing the *Agrégation* competitive exam—to visit Moscow and meet with the Russian socialists, with one of whom he would remain friends until the end of his life; a Germanophile by origin and by temperament whose reading of Hegel would break ground in philosophy courses in conservative France; a lifelong pacifist opposed to all wars, and an advocate for the rapprochement between France and Germany, and this in spite of the devastating rivalries and wars that too often disrupted the intellectual harmony between two undeniably fraternal countries with similar and complementary cultural and scientific pursuits; a European humanist long before the Treaty of Rome who would have supported the EU's open borders, sharing of intellectual resources, publishing and library partnerships to promote a high level of intellectual life and perhaps outside a system of elite schools dominated by competition. His *Weltanschauung* and the world we inhabit today are unquestionably related, and it seems appropriate to discover, or rediscover, today the vision that Lucien Herr hoped would form the basis of more just and equitable societies as early as 1900.

In order to better acquaint the reader of this thesis now being published in the United States, *Lucien Herr—Librarian*, it will be useful to briefly introduce Herr in terms of the historical, political, and intellectual context of France in the second half of the 19th century and the beginning of the 20th, and to introduce a few notions concerning the French education system, the military, and several historical events which help make sense of the complex role played by Lucien Herr during his lifetime not only as a librarian, but as a committed intellectual and socialist.

The formative years—from Alsace to the rue d'Ulm

Lucien Herr was born in Altkirch in 1864, and would survive the invasion of Alsace by the Prussian army in 1870 and their victory over the French the next year, although he lost both his mother and paternal grandfather, who died of illness during the occupation. Moreover, in the peace treaty between the two belligerents in 1871, Alsace, along with parts of Lorraine, was annexed into the *Deutsches Reich* (known also as Imperial Germany; historically this was the second German empire, after the medieval Holy Roman Empire, and preceding the Third Reich which lasted from 1939 to 1945). Jean Herr chose to remain a citizen of France, and the family of three—Lucien, his father and his older brother—were obliged by the terms of the treaty to leave Altkirch by December 31, 1872. They settled eventually in Vitry-le-François in the Marne *Département*, east of Paris. The Franco-Prussian War and its aftermath would significantly mark French social, political and military attitudes towards Germany for the next forty years.

Herr was raised in a strict Catholic family, in a devoutly Catholic region of France. His father Jean was a schoolmaster who taught school and also helped develop, for the French Ministry of Public Instruction (today known as the Ministry of National Education), what was known as *enseignement primaire supérieur* from 1833–1941, which would become the French middle school, with a heavy emphasis on mathematics, science and professional instruction adapted to the needs of each region. His mother Marie-Anne Gilardoni was the descendant of Italian immigrants who had settled in the region at the beginning of the 19th century as tile manufacturers. Lucien grew up accustomed to his father's lack of warmth and his rigorous educational methods: Jean Herr obliged his two sons, for example, to attend Mass every morning before school, even in deep snow and freezing weather. Although Lucien showed great religious fervor as a child, his religious impulses gave way to secular anticlericalism, informed by his growing intellectual development towards rationalism, intellectualism and the scientific method, further encouraged by his four years in the Lycée Louis-le-Grand in Paris. In 1883 he was admitted to the École Normale Supérieure where he chose philosophy as his major course of study. The thesis published below outlines Herr's intellectual itinerary, but suffice it to point out here that between the end of the Franco-Prussian War, with the fall of the Second Empire, and Herr's years as a Normalien, 1883–1886, the French national educational system was going through a painful transition from a Church- and clergy-influenced system to a rational and scientific institution that would eventually fulfill the Cartesian ideals of the original French revolutionaries at the end of the 18th century. But when Herr first entered the ENS, there were still strong restrictions in the Ministry of Public Instruction about what type of science was to be taught—Darwin, for example, was still proscribed by some of the ministerial personnel left from the imperial régime. Only the "natural science"—that all human beings were created by God as described in the Bible—was to be taught, and certainly not that *Homo sapiens* had evolved from primates. The ENS itself was gradually moving away from this archaic and archconservative model and the model they looked towards was the German university, which explains why a Normalien could be sent after graduation for one academic year to a German university to observe what was going on, particularly in the departments of philosophy, science, and languages and literature. The young graduate would then write up a report that was carefully read and analyzed by the directors of the ENS who would implement as many reforms in their courses as possible.

But how was it possible that students from one of France's most elite and highly respected schools were travelling to the country of France's enemies? This is only a seeming paradox. There have always been strong intellectual, artistic, cultural, scientific, and personal ties between the two countries—indeed, historically, France and Germany were countries that were given to Charlemagne's descendents as the Holy Roman Empire, and the forces that have divided the two countries have never been as strong as those that have brought them together in common pursuits.

The Franco-Prussian War and the fall of the Second French Empire[2]

The Second World War would not have taken place had Germany not been saddled with the impossible reparations payments imposed by the French in the Treaty of Versailles in 1918, which resulted in Germany seeking revenge against France. Those treaty terms, and the First World War, would not have taken place had France not sought revenge against Germany after the humiliating defeat inflicted on them after the disastrous Franco-Prussian War of 1870–71, when Germany claimed the iron-rich French regions of Alsace and Lorraine and saddled France with reparations payments amounting to 5 billion francs.[3] The Franco-Prussian War would not have taken place had the united and technologically advanced country of Germany not sought revenge on France after the Napoleonic wars of conquest between 1803 and 1815.

---

2   France initially invaded the Northern German States on the basis of erroneous assumptions: that Austria and the Southern German states would align with the French against Prussia (they did not); that the French army was not only technologically equal to the German armies but that maintaining defensive positions would suffice to defeat the Germans (neither proved to be true: the German armies were both much more disciplined and had much more advanced artillery; and they overwhelmed the French forces in the two major battles, Metz and Sedan, in mere weeks); finally, the French newspaper and popular responses to Bismarck in the form of intense Germanophobia and warmongering—emotional and over-excited reactions—were used to justify the French incursion into Saarbrücken (a major logistical and strategic error that would actually cost the French the entire war just months later). The Prussian army invaded and defeated the French in what was perceived as a crushing, humiliating blow a little over six months later in January 1871.

3   Based on the 1875 value of gold, 1 French franc = 0.2903225 grams of gold; the current price of gold (August 2019) is approximately $1499.09 per ounce, making an 1875 ounce of gold worth $14.99. The 5 Bn FrFranc reparations imposed on France in 1871would be worth some US$75 billion today.

The roots of the French defeat in 1871 lie nonetheless in choices made by the then-emperor of France, Louis-Napoléon Bonapart. He had initially been democratically elected as the first President of France after the 1848 French revolution overthrew the constitutional monarchy of Louis-Philippe I, the "King of the French", from July 26, 1830[4] until early 1848. This liberal constitutional monarchy (known as the "July Monarchy") began with the overthrow of the last French Bourbon king, Charles X, and was brought about by an alliance of the people of Paris with the French "Republicans"[5] and the liberal-thinking bourgeoisie. However, political, economic and social turmoil in France and elsewhere in Europe doomed the July Monarchy, and in 1848 a second French revolution took place to abolish the monarchy and return to the democratic and electoral form of government that had initially been the goal of the revolutionaries in 1789. The first French Presidential election was held in December 1848. The nephew of Napoléon Bonapart was elected president of France for four years. But in 1852, instead of stepping down as president as he was legally obliged to do, he seized power and proclaimed himself—as had his uncle—Emperor of France at the head of the Second French Empire. Although he was actually a very good businessman, and he sought to encourage scientific and technological progress in France during his years in power, he would ultimately bring about the defeat of the French army as a result of his government's fundamental Germanophobia and incapacity to understand the imperialistic intentions of Otto von Bismarck.

This situation was significant in what would eventually lead to, first, a complete schism between French intellectuals and the French military establishment, culminating in the Dreyfus Affair[6],

---

4   This period was known as the "July Monarchy"; the title "King of the French", as opposed to "King of France", marks his role as a "people's king".

5   This term in French political history and philosophy is concerned with the values of the *République française* as originally set out by the 1789 French Revolution. It bears no resemblance to the term "Republican" in US political history and political theory.

6   See below.

and second, ongoing cooperation, in spite of the military establishment, between the most advanced French and German academic and scientific institutions. This anomaly was fully comprehended by Lucien Herr and much of what he worked for, as a student, then *agrégé,* then librarian at the École Normale Supérieure, then militant and committed socialist in France, was a direct result of his having understood the inferiority and scandalous ineptitude of, probably, not only the French military institutions but *all* military institutions compared to a society of just citizens engaged in continuous improvement of education and knowledge-sharing as the proper object of the Republic.

The Franco-Prussian War of course directly affected Lucien Herr, as mentioned above. The losses of his mother, grandfather and his Alsatian home marked his childhood indelibly. He was a lifelong pacifist and a staunch proponent of pan-European cooperation, particularly in terms of educational cooperation and sharing of publications between France and Germany. To the extent that his lifelong job at the ENS library allowed him to procure German periodicals and books, he strengthened the links between German publishers and his own library from 1888 until his death in 1926. This included a significant effort to acquire German scientific books and publications that had been published from 1914–1918.

The aftermath of the Franco-Prussian War on French society brought some devastating events and changed attitudes in France. Not only was civil war a direct result of the French defeat in the form of the French Commune (1871), but there were also tangible negative after-shocks in the military establishment. Some French generals and military personnel developed a long-lasting hatred of all things German in a movement known as "Boulangism"—this also affected the most conservative French citizens, particularly among the upper classes and the *haute bourgeoisie.* The movement was characterized by reactionary and right-wing attitudes including a desire for military revenge against Germany and the rejection of democratic and parliamentary forms of government. It is probably not too far-fetched to imagine that the Boulangists would have embraced a military junta in France by the end of the 19th century.

One positive outcome of the French defeat was that it forced the intellectual class in France to carry out beneficial soul-searching into the reasons for German technological superiority. They reached the stark realization that French universities had allowed themselves to lag far behind in science, technology, economic theory, and the social and political sciences. From the 1870s on there would be increasing improvements to bring the level of instruction and research up to the level of German universities. Herr himself would not only experience the tension between the "old order" and a new and modern form of analytical and critical thinking in his courses at ENS, but after the obligatory voyage to Berlin to observe the university and write his report, he would dedicate his entire career at two libraries to improving the quality of the publications and media in his institutions for the benefit of the students who came after him.

Écoles Normales Supérieures, the **agrégation**

Founded in Year III (1794) of the first French Revolution, the original École Normale Supérieure (ENS) was created as the normal [teacher training] school and core institution of a centralized national education system for the purpose of providing professional pedagogical training for *lycée*[7] professors. Over time, the ENS has developed into what it is at present, namely a graduate-study level institution for producing not only university professors and senior civil servants, but also diplomats, ministers, judges and magistrates, senior managers in State offices, directors of research laboratories, directors and publishers for scientific, literary, and political

---

7   The French *lycée* is comparable to a high school in that the diploma, the *baccalauréat*, is usually obtained around age 18. Traditionally this educational institution included students aged 12–18, in grades that are numbered in descending order, i.e. *sixième* [6th grade], *cinquième* [7th grade], *quatrième* [8th grade], *troisième* [H.S. freshman], *seconde* [H.S. sophomore], *première* [H.S. junior], and the final year, *Terminale* [H.S. senior]. Today in France, students aged 12–15 attend a *collège* [middle school], and only the three final years of instruction are considered as the *lycée*. The exam itself (the *baccalauréat*, referred to as *le bac*) is now taken during the last two years, *première* and *terminale*.

research, and representatives and senators in French government. Today, along with the principal École Normal Supérieure in the rue d'Ulm in Paris (where Herr studied and became the librarian), there are three other ENSes located in Cachan, Lyons and Rennes. An ENS today is both a *grande école* and a university. The curricula of the four ENSes are slightly different, as those of Cachan and Rennes concentrate on the applied sciences and technology, the social sciences, business management and foreign languages other than Latin and Greek.

The *agrégation* is a competitive examination in the French public school system. Created in 1766 under King Louis XV, it was intended to certify professors both for the *lycée* and the universities after the Jesuits were banned from France. Those who pass the exam become French civil servants and are guaranteed tenured teaching jobs, if they so choose.

L'affaire Dreyfus, 1894–1906

The Dreyfus Affair was a French-German military espionage scandal that degenerated into a major political and governmental crisis at the end of the 19th and beginning of the 20th centuries. In September 1894, the French foreign intelligence services, who had an agent in the Imperial German embassy, came into possession of a handwritten note from a French officer addressed to Major Schwartzkoppen, the German military attaché, with a promise to provide various military secrets to the Germans. A handwriting analysis seemed to find positive identification between the writing on the note and that of Captain Alfred Dreyfus, a Polytechnician[8] of Alsatian Jewish origin who was attached to the 2nd office of the French Army Headquarters in the War Ministry. Dreyfus was arrested on 15 October 1894, found guilty of treason after a closed trial during which much of the evidence was withheld from the

---

8   Like the École Normale Supérieure, l'École Polytechnique—known also by its nickname "X"—is another French *grande école* founded during the French Revoution at the end of the 18th c. to train an elite class of engineers.

defense, his sword broken and insignia stripped from his uniform in a public degradation display, and he was sentenced to life imprisonment on Devil's Island off the coast of Guiana, a French colony in South America. Dreyfus proclaimed his innocence from the outset, and although the evidence against him was circumstantial and tenuous at best, the entire French political class sided with the military court's decision concerning his guilt.

By 1896 proof had come to light that Dreyfus was innocent in this affair: Georges Picquart, head of French military counter-intelligence services, was able to certify that the real traitor who had passed the documents to the Germans was Major Ferdinand Walsin Esterhazy, but the General Staff refused to listen and instead assigned Picquart to a post in North Africa. By 1897 Dreyfus's family—who lacked neither financial means nor connections in the government—had petitioned the President of the French Senate, who took their petition very seriously, and three months later declared that there had been a miscarriage of justice and Dreyfus was completely innocent. In 1898 two major events precipitated what would turn into a kind of non-belligerent civil war in France: Esterhazy was acquitted of treason by a military tribunal—to the acclamations of the conservatives and the nationalists; and Emile Zola published his famous open letter to the President of France, "*J'accuse*" which rallied the entire French intellectual class behind Dreyfus.

This complex affair could simply have been classed as a military imbroglio, and in fact Dreyfus could even have been retried and liberated without much more ado, had there not been a certain growing schism within French society itself ever since the country's defeat and loss of territory at the hands of the Germans in 1870–71. On the one hand, the conservatives, the military and the Catholic Church (and this group included the monarchists, as well, still hoping that either monarchy or empire would rise again) held a palpable grudge against Germany and wished for nothing better than another opportunity to avenge their loss. This would in fact become reality in the form of World War I, and particularly the harsh monetary terms inflicted on a defeated Germany in the Treaty of Versailles. But in the meantime their wish had found its personification in the form of General Georges Ernest Boulanger (nicknamed

"Général Revanche", or "General Revenge"), a populist who at first championed the causes of ordinary soldiers and the working-class and who—to the surprise of the established political classes—became extremely popular during elections in the Third Republic in 1886, and at the height of his popularity there were fears that he would simply provoke a coup d'état and seize power for himself. Proclaiming a doctrine of "the three R's"—Revenge (on Germany), Revision (of the French Constitution), and Restoration (of the monarchy)—he rallied people to his cause which came to be known as *le boulangisme*. However, he would eventually show his true colors as a staunch conservative and even monarchist when he sought—and obtained—the backing of the Bonapartists and the House of Orléans. In the end he was involved in personal scandals and left France for Great Britain. Although he himself was not successful politically, it was evident that a current of French society was deeply attracted to non-elitist, non-intellectual, and non-establishment individuals over many of the politicians of the Third Republic, and le boulangisme left lingering traces that would come to be identified as proto-fascist and extreme-right movements—some of which are still evident in France (and other countries in Europe) today.

However, Boulanger and his ideas did not convince all of the French, and the Dreyfusards, or "républicains" (the equivalent of the French left), would prevail in the end. And it was here that Lucien Herr played a decisive role in putting into motion the necessary forces that would release Dreyfus and reintegrate him into the French Army. He would play this role as he did everything: with incredible conviction and commitment, and with discretion. But he hid nothing, and those who knew him would say later that it was enough to simply listen to him state the facts in the Dreyfus case to be completely won over to the Dreyfusards, not because it was Herr persuading them, but because Herr simply spoke the truth with such powerful intelligence.[9] To begin with, as mentioned above, the family of Dreyfus—who knew that he had been falsely

---

9   Charles Andler, *La Vie de Lucien Herr (1864–1926)*, Paris, Maspero, 1932, pp. 145–51.

accused in place of another—had rallied behind Alfred's brother Mathieu, who had sought the help of Bernard Lazare, a journalist and a friend of Herr. As soon as Herr had seen the proof of the innocence of Dreyfus (the comparison of the handwriting on the note with letters from Dreyfus demonstrated beyond a doubt that the handwriting was not the captain's), he drew up a list of Normaliens—almost all of whom he had known either as classmates or as students taking out books from "his" library at the ENS—to be contacted in order to galvanize public support for Dreyfus. As the authors of one of the rare monographs on Herr stated: "The Dreyfus Affair was the high point in the life of Lucien Herr. Here his multiple activities, up to then separated and kept in different compartments, converged. The librarian, the university intellectual, the militant [socialist], the journalist became one man. Dreyfusard: this term included all the others. Herr became a Dreyfusard, as a man of science and as a militant socialist. And behind him, the entire French intelligentsia of the École Normale Supérieure and the Sorbonne followed in his steps."[10]

Socialism in 19th century France

At the same time that Herr was assiduously exercising his role as the ENS librarian, he was also known as one of the earliest supporters of socialism in France, having travelled to Germany and Russia in 1886–87 to meet members of the Internationale, some of whom would become life-long friends. He published brief reports and comments for every new book published (and not only in French—in German, English and in several other languages as well) using his own name—but he was meanwhile publishing numerous articles in the earliest French socialist newspapers using the pseudonym "Pierre Breton". A life-long pacifist, he opposed all wars.

From Herr's own family background—his father's modest position as a middle-school teacher, his mother's family who

---

10 D. Lindenberg, P.A. Meyer, *Lucien Herr: Le Socialism et son destin*, Paris, Calmann-Lévy, 1977, p. 141 [my translation].

were manufacturers, both sides descendents of farmers and people who lived off the land in earlier generations—and from his widespread reading and natural inclinations towards rationalism and the scientific method, his political choices as a socialist in late 19th-century France were clear. There were sharp class distinctions in France that Herr would have observed just from his position as a student at the ENS. He attended a school intended for the sons of the well-to-do bourgeoisie before obtaining positions as *haut fonctionnaires* (senior officials) in the French administration and bureaucracy, or as fully tenured university professors, or officials in government or foreign service. However, from his father's own job in the past, when he helped to develop the curriculum for the precursors of the French professional training lycées, Herr had understood the need to more fully integrate the sons of workers and farmers into French society through proper education. Moreover, Herr himself of course benefited from the élite education he received at the ENS: but he chose not to use this to place himself into a comfortable sinecure for the rest of his life after obtaining his diplomas and degrees. This probably explains his intense dedication to a task that others might have considered mundane and lowly, and certainly devoid of personal ambition and public recognition or personal glory.

It is not possible to go into the full depth and breadth of Herr's socialist commitments and ideals in the space of this brief introduction, but it will suffice to say that through his actions in the library—the introduction of the complete works of Hegel, Marx, Engels, Darwin, the English political philosophers, among others, along with his zeal in reviewing every single scientific, literary, and philosophical publication and periodical that appeared in the years while he was at the library in order to separate the wheat from the chaff and alert readers to the books and journal articles that were necessary reading, and those that could be set aside as worthless—he provided a solid intellectual foundation for the hundreds of future senior civil servants and even leaders in French society, not only in politics but in letters and the sciences in terms of the books he put into their hands and the advice he gave to them when he had lunch with them in the school cafeteria every day.

It is this collaborative effort, unceasing and always directed at giving students, not answers, but the keys to unlock their own doors, that allowed Herr to pursue a better form of social action than he had found in the *Parti Ouvrier Socialiste Révolutionnaire* or the *Section Française de l'Internationale Ouvrière*.[11] He helped found the newspaper l'*Humanité* with Jean Jaurès and others, which was Socialist in its beginnings in 1904; although it is now the official medium of the French Communist Party, it still exists to this day. Finally, Herr was one of the two official Socialist party members on the board of the *Ligue des Droits de l'Homme* (Human Rights League), founded in 1904 in France in order to defend Captain Dreyfus, and based on and adhering strictly to the *Déclaration des droits de l'homme et du citoyen* of 1789.

Herr did not publish his translation of Hegel (he destroyed it instead), he did not seek a prestigious public position, and he did not leave behind him an opus of research, philosophical thought or even bibliographic methodology to pass on to future librarians. In the final analysis, Lucien Herr was too lucid, and too conscious of the ultimate irony of his own situation. Every student who passes the fierce competitive examination to enter the École Normale Supérieure knows that she or he will not leave the school, graduate degree and *agrégation* in hand, in order to serve the people. They know that they are going to serve the French State. Herr was no exception: but like Melville's Bartleby, he quietly murmured his "I would prefer not to", not to a blank wall, but among the bookshelves of his intellectual abode in the library of the rue d'Ulm. He chose intelligent, informed, conscious silence—which was his way of remaining in service to "the State" while at the same time performing the counter-service of bringing into the library the books that the State University would not yet allow to be taught. And he continued to expand the services and functions of the library as if it were the heart of a truly democratic society where education was available for all and freely accessible. He accepted only one other

---

11   The two branches of socialist political parties to which Herr adhered after about 1889, so just a year after his appointment as librarian at the ENS.

mission in all his years as the ENS librarian, which is described in the thesis: he accepted the job as the head of the Musée Péda-gogique (the precursor of the INRP—*Institut national de recherche pédagogique*), which included a very large collection of images. He developed a lending system so that schools all over France could use all of the resources in the MP. And he remained a steadfast social-ist, convinced that political theory was not what was needed to im-prove the lives of ordinary people—militant action was, and in his own way he carried out that action.

Let us end here with his own words, from 1888: "Insurrec-tion, revolt, or in simple terms, examination and critical analysis—this is a our duty, and not just for exceptional cases. All the time."[12]

---

12   Lindenberg & Meyer, *op.cit.*, p. 315 [my translation].

Translator's Introduction

Tegan Raleigh

Lucien Herr was a librarian, book critic, mentor, and politically engaged intellectual. He was also a translator. Yet his most ambitious
translation project, what was to be the first complete edition in French
of Hegel's *Phänomenologie des Geistes* (*Phenomenology of the Spirit/
Mind*), never saw the light of day: Herr was dissatisfied with his translation and it was never published; *Phénoménologie de l'esprit*, translated by Jean Hyppolite, did not appear until 1941, nearly 150 years after its original publication in Hegel's German. Potentially it was the
difficulty of Hegel's language that led Herr to be displeased with his
translation, for Herr highly esteemed clarity in scholarship. He was
scathing in his criticisms of those, for example, with "a remarkable
banality of mind [...] expressed in unbearably ambitious and affected language."[1] Though Hegel's writings were certainly not banal, his
notoriously abstruse writing style has led to struggles for generations
of translators attempting to make his ideas lucid and comprehensible.

Herr's activities as librarian as well as translator were a part
of the bigger picture that he had of intellectual progress, which involved making knowledge available to all. This aim of democra-
tizing knowledge is consistent with the reader-oriented translation
methodology he outlines in the introduction to his translation of

---

1 Cited by Grandmougin, with bibliographic material in footnote 83.

the correspondence between Schiller and Goethe. Here, he explains that such a methodology entails finding equivalents in his contemporary idiom for philosophical terminology from the turn of the nineteenth century and making stylistic changes from the German in order to better accommodate readers of French. For the present translation, I likewise aimed for a style that is readerly, accounting in particular for conventions of Anglophone scholarship so as to best communicate the vivid, incisive, and lucid tone of the text in French by Grandmougin who, like Herr, wears her erudition lightly.

Grandmougin positions Herr within the context of the emergence of a new kind of intellectual in France and links developments of the *esprit* to advances in *science,* and vice versa. For the English translation of Grandmougin's intellectual portrait of Herr, these two terms required some consideration, especially given their centrality to the political and social movements of the time. Herr's notions of progress and intellectual freedom were linked to the philosopher who proved so difficult for him translate: Hegel. In his 2019 translation of *Phänomenologie,* Terry Pinkard noted that the German *Geist,* which is generally *esprit* in French, can lead to some ambiguity in English. Hegel's work, for example, appears in English as *Phenomenology of Spirit* (as in Pinkard's edition) as well as, less frequently, *Phenomenology of Mind.* Because of Herr's indebtedness to Hegelianism, "spirit" as a translation of *esprit* rather than "mind" would have the advantage of being the same word frequently used to render the German *Geist.* However, there is no one-to-one correspondence between *esprit* and "spirit," and a phrase such as "the indoctrination of the spirits of the École" (rather than "minds of the École") could be misleading, particularly given Herr's staunch opposition to the spiritualism of his contemporaries and colleagues like Léon Ollé-Laprune. Thus, in the present translation of Grandmougin's work, the French *esprit* is often closer to the English "mind," though in passages where *esprit* is explicitly linked to consciousness and the intellect, leaving less room for misinterpretation, the translation treats "mind" and "spirit" as interchangeable. Meanwhile, I chose "spirit," as a word referring to character or orientation rather than to a soul, in order to translate, for example, *esprit anarchique* ("anarchist spirit") that Léon Blum refers to having possessed prior to embracing socialism.

In French, the word *science*, like the German *Wissenschaft*, frequently designates scholarship or the pursuit of knowledge in general, whereas in English the term today primarily refers to fields of study based upon observation and experiment such as biology, physics, and chemistry, or the "hard sciences," as well as "soft sciences" like sociology, psychology, and anthropology. The German term for the humanities is, in fact, *Geisteswissenschaft*, which is literally "science of the mind/spirit," while in French the term is *sciences humaines*. Therefore, in French and German, there is not such a hard and fast distinction between the humanities and the sciences, given that the terms for "humanities" actually contain the respective terms for "science." While the *Oxford English Dictionary* does provide several definitions for "science" as knowledge or the pursuit of knowledge, it qualifies them as archaic. For the purposes of this translation, I therefore generally translated the word *science* as "scholarship" and *scientifique* as "scholarly" or "academic."

For terminology related to the curation and maintenance of libraries, I consulted Grandmougin herself; I am also indebted to Judith Crews, the author of the general introduction, for her comments and suggestions.

Lucien Herr—Socialist Librarian of the French Third Republic

"The library at the Ecole represents all of my dreams and my ambitions. This is the only thing I want, and it's what I've dreamed of and have wanted for years. I don't view the librarian position as temporary, but rather full-time and permanent. Are there other conditions you consider necessary? I commit in advance: I am prepared to do anything."

It was in these unusual terms that Lucien Herr submitted his application for the position of librarian of the Ecole Normale Supérieure (ENS) to Georges Perrot, the school's director, on December 11, 1887.[1] The anxious and urgent tone leaves no doubt as to the crucial importance he attributed to this position. Herr was a recent *agrégé* in philosophy and had just come back from Germany. Like so many of the highest-ranking graduates of the ENS at that time, he had been sent there to draw up a report on the situation of philosophy at the German universities. Upon returning to France, he experienced a kind of mystical crisis, as related in the biography of Herr by Charles Andler, Herr's closest friend and fellow socialist. The crisis lasted several months, and during this time Herr read a great deal and broke off contact with his friends. It was at the end

---

1   This letter is in the collection conserved at the French national archives. It is reproduced in its entirety in Appendix 1.

of this mysterious period that he made the decision to devote his life to the ENS library.

Paradoxically, it was precisely this passionate view of librarianship as a vocation that initially cost Herr the job. In a letter dated April 1888, Perrot confided to Joseph Bédier, another candidate for the position, that he had designed the librarian position as a temporary convenience that would allow a recent *agrégé* to "take advantage of the salary and the free time that goes along with it so as to be able to finish a dissertation or a book."[2] This was, all in all, quite the opposite of the life project that Herr had set forth. Andler recalls that it took the intervention of Louis Liard, then Directeur de l'Enseignement Supérieur (Director of Higher Education) in France, to secure Herr's appointment.

Herr in fact refused most of the positions he was offered, unlike his predecessors Jules Chantepie de Dézert and Alfred Rébelliau. These two *agrégés* had left the ENS library after a few years for positions as the Inspection Générale (General Inspectorate) of university libraries and the Chair of French literature at the Université de Rennes, respectively. Herr only accepted the position as director of the Musée Pedagogique (Pedagogical Museum), a polymorphous establishment, in 1916, and he combined his duties there with those of the ENS library. Officially appointed as librarian in November 1888, he remained at the ENS for 34 years until his death on May 18, 1926. In a letter to Andler dated May 20, 1925, he wrote, "I intend to remain faithful to my old task of the Ecole up until the very end."[3] The institution has never forgotten this long period of service, and the bust of Lucien Herr that was unveiled in 1928 still presides over the reading room of the Bibliothèque des Lettres today.

However, few traces of Herr remain, making it challenging to represent his life as a librarian. There is an almost complete absence of primary sources directly related to the library and even fewer for

2   Letter to Joseph Bédier, cited by Charles Andler, *La Vie de Lucien Herr*, François Maspero, Paris, 1977, p. 71.

3   Lucien Herr collection at Sciences Po, LH2, dossier 4.

the Musée Pédagogique (MP), which presents difficulties in reconstructing Herr's career. Four archives are available as sources of information:[4] the administrative collection conserved at the ENS library on the rue d'Ulm; the ENS archives; the MP collection donated to the Archives Nationales (French national archives); and the Lucien Herr collection at the historical center at the Institut d'études politiques de Paris (Paris Institute of Political Studies), or Sciences Po.

These collections consist primarily of acquisition and lending records, catalogues, and invoices. Documents containing references by Herr to his activities at the library or at the museum and communicating his vision for these two institutions are quite rare. The collections are essentially comprised of the periodical reports Herr addressed to the ENS director or the Ministre de l'Instruction publique (Minister of Public Education). There are a few select letters that make it possible to define Herr's ambitions for these two institutions as a means for disseminating knowledge and culture. The vast majority of those who have written about Herr, including Andler, refer to these reports when discussing Herr's role at the ENS. To the best of our knowledge, reports concerning the MP have not been used in order to reconstruct Herr's activity there.[5]

An additional methodological challenge results from the fact that Herr's writing was limited almost exclusively to correspondence, brief commentaries about new books, proof corrections, and fragments of political reflections. Neither for himself nor for professional librarians did Herr write down the foundations or the major methodological principles for librarianship, despite the fact that these were his lifelong preoccupations. In his biography of Herr, Andler laments that such a fertile mind should have produced so very little to focus instead on reading, advising, and classifying the works of others. This lamentation recurs as a leitmotif. In terms of works signed by Herr in his own name, there is only *Choix d'écrits I et II* (*Selected Writings I and II*), which is a collection of fragments

4   The annual report details the contents of this collection.

5   Given that direct sources about Herr's activities at the library are rare, several of these documents are reproduced in the appendices.

compiled in 1932 by Mario Roques (1875–1961), a professor of history who was a friend of Herr's and a fellow Dreyfusard of the first hour. These brief writings offer no clarifications regarding the library as an institution. It is also important to note Herr's unbending severity regarding his own work: having translated Hegel's *Phänomenologie des Geistes* (*Phenomenology of the Spirit*), he judged his own translation to be unsatisfactory and destroyed it.[6]

Only a very limited number of works about Herr have been published. There are just two monographs: Andler's biography-tribute, which charts the various aspects of Herr's life in very knowledgeable but at the same time rather emotional terms, and the book by Daniel Lindenberg and Pierre-André Meyer entitled *Lucien Herr, le Socialisme et son destin* (*Lucien Herr, Socialism, and Its Destiny*),[7] which retraces his political commitment as a socialist, pacifist, and Dreyfusard. In addition, there is the Andler-Herr correspondence edited by Antoinette Blum,[8] with the majority of the letters offering comments about university life: the *agrégation* competition, nominations, course offerings, publications, etc. Several articles and monograph chapters, as well as the frequent allusions to Herr in numerous issues of *Histoire des Intellectuels* (*History of Intellectuals*) attest to his influence, on the one hand, while simultaneously pointing to the lacunae that pose obstacles to an accurate and comprehensive analysis of his life, on the other.

Last but not least, a vast body of accounts about Herr from recollections, letters, obituaries, and speeches delivered after his death tells us about the librarian at the ENS. However, these statements are very much biased in terms of personal viewpoints, politics, or social conventions and are thus to be approached with caution. More often than not, they are distinctly hagiographic in tone.

---

6   Etienne Verley, "Lucien Herr et le positivisme," *Romantisme*, no. 21–22, p. 221.

7   Daniel Lindenberg and Pierre-André Meyer: *Lucien Herr, le Socialisme et son destin*, Calmann-Lévy, Paris, 1977.

8   Antoinette Blum: *Correspondance entre Charles Andler et Lucien Herr 1891–1926*, Presses de l'Ecole Normale Supérieure, Paris, 1992.

Herr seems to have aroused passionate attachments and acknowledgments as well as effusive admiration. There are also occasional notes of distrust and bitterness linked to his influence on young minds, though these are comparatively rare.

It is therefore possible to say that while "Herr the socialist" is rather well-known, "Herr the librarian," on the other hand, is a centrally important but unknown figure who has acquired an almost fictional dimension: a mysterious hero of astounding erudition who spoke all languages, read everything, and gave up the brilliant academic career that seemed to await him just so he could devote himself to an obscure job in the library. A paradoxical figure emerges, since there is both the myth of Herr that is rich in firsthand accounts as well as a curious lack of detail. Research about Herr as librarian therefore requires the methodological rigor that is indispensible when bringing together sources of varying levels of reliability. The statements about Herr help to gauge his influence on the generations that followed him and account for the Herr "myth" that is so central to his legend. They can be especially fruitful when they are brought into dialogue with Herr's own writings which, despite being fragmented, constitute a corpus of solid primary sources.

First of all, his brief book commentaries form an integral whole that is both complete and coherent. The philosophical fragments gathered in his *Choix d'écrits* (*Selected Writings*) under the title *Le Progrès et l'affranchissement* (*Progress and Liberation*) are another important source for understanding the decidedly metaphysical foundations of his dedication to librarianship. The annual reports concerning the MP written in Herr's hand and maintained at the French national archives provide useful information about the development of new activities in the library world. His correspondence is also informative: this shifting, polymorphous resource is a trove of clues and brusque assertions as well as lacunae and silences. By bringing all these sources together along with the available historical documents, it has been possible to detect recurring echoes. Little by little, the full image of a librarian's career, cohesive and deliberate, comes to light. Taking care not to overinterpret, the task of the present study has been to build up a network of connections capable of restoring the lost memories of at least a part of what Lucien Herr represented as a librarian.

Proceeding in this manner, we are not looking for the practical aspects of library management as seen from within and through clearly defined objectives. This was accomplished by Herr's contemporaries, Ernest Coyecque for public access to reading and Paul Otlet for documentation and record-keeping, for example. Rather, what comes to light is a very personal idea of the librarian's activity that extends well beyond the stacks of the ENS. Herr so insistently sought to become the director of the ENS library because he envisioned his library as the heart of a certain concept of society itself. The life that Andler described as "so ramified, so secret, so profound" had as its focal point the library, a strategic place for the creation and advancement of a shared intellectual life.

Lucien Herr, Librarian

The Foundations of Commitment

It is appropriate, with Herr, to speak of librarianship as a form of commitment. He dedicated himself entirely to his profession, which for him assumed the form of a vocation. Sketching Herr's intellectual and ideological portrait makes it possible to draw out some of the main features and to demonstrate how Herr's library was at the center of a society undergoing profound transformation.

Context

The Intellectual Polarization of Society

The last two decades of the nineteenth century were marked by a strong polarization of the intellectual world. A philosophical and political geography that defined the left by a reformist drive and the right by conservative values was in the process of establishing itself. Three great historians of intellectual history—Michel Winock,

Pascal Ory and Jean-François Sirenelli—have found an illustration of this ever-increasing divide in the novel by Maurice Barrès (1862–1923) entitled *Les Déracinés* (*The Uprooted*), which is the first volume of the national trilogy *Roman de l'Energie (Novel of Energy)*.[9] This novel's main character, Paul Bouteiller, is a philosophy instructor from the provinces who receives a scholarship and goes to Paris with some of his students. His secret hope is to become a *député* (minister). He is the prototype of the intellectual of the *République*, heralding the breed so despised by Barrès: that of the *agrégé* who enters politics and plays a leading role in the "République des professeurs" ("Republic of teachers"), claiming upward social mobility based on merit, knowledge, and academic accomplishments. A pacifist and universalist, defender of *républicain* values, his opportunism is revealed by his race to enter the *Chambre*, where he ultimately finds himself tarnished by the scandals of a corrupt parliamentary class. In contrast stands the purity of the author's moralism, affirming a nationalism that is fixed in roots, homeland, and the military establishment. With his political engagement as leader of the anti-Dreyfusard camp in late 1897, Barrès enjoyed a formidable prestige among members of the intellectual class until the end of the century. His anti-conformity and the great enthusiasm for his novels from the late 1880s made him an intellectual leader for young people rising against the standards imposed by tradition. Léon Blum himself consulted with the "master" to try to gather the Dreyfusards around him. It was a moment of rupture and of radicalization. But this suffices to explain Barrès's influence, and his ability to personify the political right among intellectuals.

At the same time, on the political terrain, Boulangism served as a catalyst for the enemies of the Third Republic. General Boulanger or "General Revenge" was a spearhead of antiparliamentarianism. His supporters saw in him an opportunity to initiate profound constitutional revisions or even overthrow the *République*

---

9   On this subject, see the first chapters of: Winock, Michel: *Le Siècle des Intellectuels*, Seuil, Paris, 1999, and de Ory, Pascal and Sirenelli, Jean-François: *Les Intellectuels en France, de l'Affaire Dreyfus à nos jours*, Perrin, 1987.

with a coup d'état. His military warmongering energized those who were disappointed by parliamentary inertia following the traumatic defeat of 1871 and hoped that France would get its revenge on Germany.

The Situation at the Ecole Normale Supérieure

Herr entered the ENS in 1883. He passed his *agrégation* at the age of 22 and became the library director two years later in 1888. This was a pivotal period for the institution and for higher education in general. According to Louis Liard (1846–1917), a Normalien and *agrégé* in philosophy who became the Directeur de l'Enseignement Supérieur (Director of Higher Education) at the Ministre de l'Instruction Publique (Ministry of Public Education) in 1884, France's defeat in 1871 was attributable to its failure to keep up with Germany intellectually. In his *Histoire de l'enseignement supérieur* (*History of Higher Education*), Liard writes that it was necessary to attend to "the recovery of higher education, because the strength of a nation resides not only with its armies, but also its specialized schools."[10]

Positivism, which was winning over the younger generation of intellectuals, was encouraged. Important progressive intellectuals such as Paul Vidal de la Blache (1845–1918), a Normalien with his *agrégation* degree in History and Geography, and Gabriel Monod (1844–1912), with his *agrégation* in History, stepped onto the scene. They became professors at the ENS in 1877 and 1879, respectively. In their teaching of history, they endeavored to introduce the critical and scientific methods that characterized instruction at the German universities. There were anti-science reactions, however, that stalled their efforts at revitalization. Reflecting French society's polarization, there was a conflict between the Ancients and the Moderns playing out at the ENS during the last decades of the nineteenth century. When Herr arrived at the ENS, the classical humanities still accounted for the lion's share of instruction. The

---

10   Louis Liard, *Histoire de l'enseignement supérieur, 1888–1894*, Volume 2, p. 337, cited by Daniel Lindenberg, op. cit., p. 29.

programs of the 1883 conferences for the *Lettres*, reproduced by Lindenberg,[11] attest to this. French, Latin and Greek accounted for eighteen of the twenty-five or twenty-six hours of lessons per week for the first and second year. Additionally, there were three hours a week for philosophy, and the professor at the time was Léon Ollé Laprune, a fierce defender of the Church and a militant, reactionary Catholic. He favored a classical education along the lines of Plato-Descartes-Leibniz-Kant and the French spiritualist tradition, ignoring the English and German philosophy of the nineteenth century such as Hegelianism. History was limited to ancient history, also three hours of classes per week. Grammar and geography were considered to be auxiliary disciplines and were not taught separately. There was no instruction dedicated to languages or the social sciences.

During his time at the ENS, Herr joined the positivist camp. There was a new generation emerging from among the students. They were politically liberal, as confirmed by their vote during the Boulangiste crisis for demonstrations against the General. Energized by German philosophy and rationalism, they rejected the spiritualism of Ollé-Laprune and the egocentric mysticism of Barrès, author of *Le Culte du Moi (The Cult of Me)*. Herr was one of rationalism's most ardent defenders. At the beginning of his text *Le progrès et l'affranchissement (Progress and Liberation),* he denounced "mystical sentimentalism" and refused to come out in favor of the "sentimentals" or the "intellectualists." The new mind, "the new state of thought" was to be a combination of "immanence, rationalism, autonomy."[12] It was from this perspective that Herr, though he was going to be a librarian, did what he could to give the social sciences their rightful place at the ENS and, most importantly, open them up to the contemporary world. The scholar at grips with the real was at the heart of the Herrian notion of the intellectual.

---

11 Daniel Lindenberg, op. cit., p. 36

12 Lucien Herr, *Choix d'écrits II, Philosophie, Histoire, Philologie*, Rieder, Paris, 1932, p. 11.

Socialism

An understanding of Herr's political involvement illuminates the different facets of his librarianship. His socialism, informed by a positivist confidence in the progressive virtues of science, gave wide berth to the role of the intellectual, who was to be in the service of knowledge and universal progress. The centrality of science and the spirit of critical inquiry in challenging dogmatic thinking created the conditions for the liberation of the mind, a necessary prerequisite to all other forms of liberation.

Prior to the first congress of socialists in 1905, called the Congrès du Globe (Congress of the Globe), the many separate factions of socialism were not always easily distinguishable. Andler determined that Herr came to socialism "very early, by 1889 at the latest."[13] This was the year that he joined the FTSF (*Féderation des Travailleurs Socialistes de France*, Federation of Socialist Workers of France), which was the "possibiliste" socialist party of Paul Brousse and Jean Allemane. When this party split in 1890, Herr and Andler followed Allemane, who then established the POSR (*Parti Ouvrier Socialiste Révolutionnaire*, Revolutionary Socialist Workers' Party). The POSR was a workers' party with union activities that advocated for general strikes as an effective means of action. Herr's choice of this party may seem paradoxical: the Allemanists were in fact very wary of the intellectual socialists, suspecting them of seeking "distinction" by attempting to rise above the common condition to court-elected positions, leaving material labor to the proletariat. They regarded electoralist ambitions with mistrust and doggedly monitored municipal appointees. Yet this requirement to remain at some remove was especially suited to a man such as Herr. Michel Winock justifies this association with his "phobia of exhibition, his refusal of a career, his taste for work out of the limelight."[14] All throughout his life, his commitment was characterized by a "refusal

---

13   Charles Andler, op. cit., p. 117.

14   Michel Winock, in *Mélanges d'histoire sociale offerts à J. Maitron*, Editions ouvrières, 1976, p. 276.

to achieve" and a modesty that was the object of universal commendation. Andler reported that in 1920, when he was publishing the first volume of his work on Nietzsche, he wanted to incude Herr's name on the cover as the second author so as to acknowledge Herr's significant contributions. Herr refused several times and the book only contains a mention of thanks in its initial pages.[15]

In his book on intellectual socialism,[16] Georges Lefranc retraced a strong ideological lineage between Herr and Pierre Lavrov (1823–1900). Lavrov was a major representative of the Russian revolutionary movement of the 1870s, and the proximity that Lefranc identifies between the two men is largely due to the role assigned to the intellectual in social progress. Lavrov assigned great importance to criticism and rational thought as the only historical driving forces capable of giving humanity access to freedom. Because they were capable of bringing forth new ideas, they served as spearheads in the fight against dogmatism. Similarly, for Herr it was theoretical thinking that completed the "practical" aspects of political engagement.

This importance accorded to the role of intellectuals, or rather of intellectual capacity itself, established a division of tasks within a society. Like Lavrov, Herr classified individuals based on their intellectual and rational faculties, and he delineates three categories in *Progrès*. The first includes those for whom reserves of prejudices remain intact, with "new ideas seated at the summit of the mental edifice without making a dent in it."[17] The second are those for whom the "new idea makes a place for itself and organizes some mental content, to a certain degree." And the third is for "those who dare to take their ideas to the limit."

This division of minds by ability was a way to gauge the part that each member would take in the liberation of the mind and hence in general progress. Indeed, if it was through the individual

---

15   Charles Andler, op. cit., p. 196.

16   Georges Lefranc: *Jaurès et le socialisme des intellectuels*, Aubier, 1968, pp 87 et seq.

17   Lucien Herr, op. cit., p. 14.

mind that the "new idea" would emerge, the deliberate organization of individual talents was to result in the advancement of the collective mind. However, it was not a natural given, in the sense that an individual would belong to one category or another indefinitely. The positivist confidence in the general march of human progress thanks to science encouraged the improvement of individual faculties through work, properly-guided training, and sound counsel. In this sense, the classification of minds contributed to the overall project by describing a "state of mind" to aim for so the greatest number of people could participate in change and ultimately strive for the creation of a socialist society.

These "beautiful minds" were to be entirely attuned to social reality. Lavrov writes that "I designate as intellectuals only those who serve to promote human solidarity, whatever the scope of their knowledge and whatever their profession. Workers who endeavor to understand better, to serve their social ideal, are far more entitled to the title of 'intellectual' than professors who write multiple books but remain strangers to all the questions of their times."[18] Herr likewise expressed his disdain for "the debauchery of erudition without a purpose." In these matters, he claimed that it was necessary to beware of the "pretty" and devote oneself to the " useful."[19] "My mind and my heart aren't there anymore," he wrote to Andler in the autumn of 1902. "I do not care enough about matters that are purely speculative; I'm only capable of being passionate about that which leads to implementation, to intellectual and social growth."[20] Herr's engagement as a librarian assumed the form of a mission: to relocate the library so that instead of remaining in a context of elegant erudition, it would rather face the world.

---

18   Cited by Georges Lefranc, op. cit., p. 81.

19   Fragments collected under the title *La Révolution sociale*, collection in the archives of the Centre d'Histoire de Sciences Po, carton LH5, dossier 1, p. 113.

20   Antoinette Blum, op. cit., letter 10, p. 64. This letter is fundamental to understanding the meaning of Herr's commitment as a librarian. The most important part is reproduced in Appendix 4.

Hegelianism

Herr's great project, which Andler lamented never saw the light of day, was Hegel in three volumes. Overwhelmed by his numerous tasks, bypassed during his visit to Germany by Hegel's rights holders who refused him access to the great philosopher's unpublished manuscripts,[21] Herr only wrote a single article, "Hegel," for the *Grande Encyclopédie* on the subject.[22] To this are added the fragments "two rough compilations" bearing the title, *Le Progrès intellectuel et l'affranchissement* (*Intellectual Progress and Liberation*) with the sub-title, *Le Progrès en conscience et en liberté* (*Progress in Conscience and Liberty*). Andler discovered these, as he himself reports in his biography,[23] and Mario Roques had them published posthumously in *Choix d'écrits de Lucien Herr*.[24] Very much tinged with Hegelianism, they constituted, according to Andler, the preliminary sketch of a mysterious, more personal work that Herr had spoken about to just a few friends and for which the Hegel translation would have served as an introduction. Andler dates the writing to 1888–1890.

Herr's Hegelianism elevated the progress of the mind to the rank of a historical driving force. While the socialist ideal of the liberation of the proletariat informed this view, it also had an even more essential dimension as a veritable philosophy of history—an understanding of the march of civilizations towards their fulfillment. Herr's text is approximately thirty pages and alternates aphorisms with developments that are considerably longer, though never in excess of two or three pages. It is an invaluable resource for

---

21   Charles Andler, op. cit., p. 64–65.

22   Marcellin Berthelot (dir.), *La Grande Encyclopédie, Inventaire raisonné des sciences, lettres et des arts*, Article "Hegel," Société anonyme de la Grande Encyclopédie, Paris, 1886–1902. This article is reproduced in its entirety in *Lucien Herr, Choix d'écrits II*, op. cit., p. 109–46.

23   Charles Andler, op. cit., p. 91.

24   Lucien Herr, op. cit., p. 9 to 47.

understanding Herr's philosophy of history and his notion of the progress of the human mind.

The text begins with an eminently Hegelian statement, situating readers within the context of a philosophy of progress and immanence:

> "There is no truth. There is no ideal realized outside of us towards which we gravitate by successive approximations; there is not a truth that our means of knowing can and must reach and appropriate, bit by bit. There is only one truth for humankind, and this is the human truth."[25]

This sentence immediately inscribes us within a rationalism that refuses all transcendence. Indeed, science does not aim to unveil a truth that has remained inaccessible because of the insufficiency of our knowledge. The human spirit is evolving, but not towards a pre-existing, superior goal. It follows its own law and progressively constructs its own truth. Herr explains this phenomenon in a beautiful passage about the liberation of the mind:

> "[Progress] is in reality the critical sentiment that is becoming, that has become, the critical mind, the reigning consciousness; it is the sovereign assurance of the mind that finally knows, as so many moments abolished and surpassed, the stages it must go through, the constraints that it has endured and has imposed on itself, the dogmas it has momentarily inhabited, the powers it has erected in front of itself, and before which it has bowed; it is… the mind finally master of itself, mocking the ghosts it had made for itself and which it had previously succumbed to in fear."[26]

---

25   Lucien Herr, op. cit., p. 13.

26   Lucien Herr, op. cit., p. 17.

For this truth, the instrument of conquest is critique, which allows the mind to free itself of dogmas and to become conscious of its own liberation, of its path towards consciousness of itself. It is the mechanism of Progress. If it is desirable, it's because it improves our lives:

> "Life is good, and the life that the progress of the mind gives us is the best and the most precious that has ever been experienced."[27]

On the human scale, progress is measured in generations, with the condition of progress being "to increase the independence of each new generation."[28] The human truth to which Herr refers and towards which the mind progresses is the movement by which the mind deliberately breaks free of historical lies and achieves its own liberation by knowing itself.

What are these deceptions, these ghosts? They are doctrine and religion, which for Herr means systems of thought that explain *faits accomplis*, justify them, and present them as natural. In other words, a doctrine "detects a state and systematizes it, explains it metaphysically. It is therefore a lie."[29] Doctrine and religion both present themselves as harmonious organizations of the real where every element is ordered. As it progresses, the mind must realize that these systems of order are not natural states but rather social and political constructions serving the interests of the few, those who are "fit." Progress manifests itself through an upsurge of "new ideas," which serve as indicators that the mind is emerging from the inertia of the past and acquiring new energy. The source of this upsurge is rather mysterious: to a certain extent, it is the defeat of old beliefs that makes it possible. A curious vitalism surrounds the description of this manifestation of the life of the mind:

---

27   Lucien Herr, op. cit., p. 16.

28   Lucien Herr, op. cit., p. 27.

29   Lucien Herr, op. cit., p. 28.

> "New ideas act … like centers of light, points of ten-
> sion, impulses around which behavior—that is, feelings
> and ideas—gradually aggregate and organize themselves
> through the natural process of psychological life."[30]

Here, there is a double functioning that is simultaneously individual and collective. While the psychological genesis of a new idea
is attributable to mere "impulses," it is crucial to identify this idea
when it manifests itself in reality beyond the individual mind, when
it is made public; for collective progress proceeds as it continuously
combines with and coordinates with other new ideas.

Finally, it is by practicing critical thought that the mind
reveals itself as being free and conscious of itself. Herr writes that
"[i]nsurrection, the revolt of the mind—or, in simple language, inspection and critique—is necessary not only in exceptional and serious cases but always,"[31] and this sentence resounds like a manifesto for a historical intellectual mission.

If Herr advocated for the library so fervently, it's because
this was the place from which he could assure his "mission" most
effectively; where he would be in contact with young minds and
burgeoning fields of scholarship. The library occupied a crucial and
strategic place in his intellectual project, which can be summed up
as liberation, or enfranchisement. Teaching the mind to be critical
in order to progress meant freedom from an old order and the advance of the human mind towards liberation. This was a task that
was both extremely ambitious and far from the limelight.

The Library of the Ecole Normale Supérieure

An Evolving Institution

At the outset, it was not a given that the ENS would have its own
library. The administrative statute that appeared in 1810, fifteen
years after the institution's establishment, contained an article

---

30   Lucien Herr, op. cit., p. 34.

31   Lucien Herr, op. cit., p. 27.

about the library. This article determined the terms for loans, which at the time were only for officials and students. But in practice, students and teachers would obtain their books from the Bibliothèque de l'Université de France located in the buildings of the imperial lycée, Louis-le-Grand. It was necessary to create the ENS library from scratch, since even the most basic materials were lacking. Its first collection consisted primarily of lexicons, classical texts, and some works of science and philosophy. Acquisitions were extremely limited and the library did not receive donations.

The ENS moved in 1814, relocating from the old *collège* of Plessis, rue Saint Jacques, to the buildings of the Congrégation du Saint Esprit, rue des Postes (today's rue Lhomond). The insufficiency of this rudimentary library became increasingly apparent. The Conseil de l'Instruction publique (the Council of Public Education) recommended that the Bibliothèque de l'Université de France be transferred to the same premises, and the ENS students would share it with those of the Sorbonne. Ultimately, it was Monsieur Guéneau de Mussy, who was the director of the ENS at that time, who prevailed with his preference for a library specifically for the ENS. Four years later, the library received concrete recognition in the form of an annual sum that was budgeted for it in its own right. The library of the Université helped it to increase its collections by providing it with its duplicate copies of books.

From then on, the library experienced periods of notable expansion (the period of the revolution of July 1830, for example), and slowdown (such as during the coup d'état of 1851). Regardless, the collections continued to develop as there was a diversification of studies at the ENS, especially in history and French literature. In addition, the library started to receive donations as well as collections bequeathed by scholars. In 1832, the state received the library of the scientist Georges Cuvier after his death; he shared the collections among different institutions, including the ENS. In 1887, a year before Herr arrived, the historian Charles Caboche bequeathed to the library a collection of 2500 volumes, rich in literature and historical memoirs. The number of books increased rapidly, from 20,000 volumes in 1845 to 60,000 in 1878, 77,000 in 1882, and more than 100,000 in 1895.

The principles of acquisition made the ENS library one for study. The library prohibited acquisitions made out of pure curiosity and avoided mass-market works for general audiences. Fustel de Coulanges (1830–1889), who directed the ENS from 1880 to 1883, just before Herr started his studies there, is reputed to have kept an attentive and severe watch over acquisitions.[32]

A very personal exercise of duties

While it is challenging to accurately reconstruct Herr's achievements as a librarian at the ENS, one thing is certain: his leadership at the library was eminently personal, and the collections were to bear his mark. A bust of Herr currently presides over the room for Lettres at the ENS library, testifying to his status as creator, or "re-creator." Georges Canguilhem, who arrived at the ENS in 1924 and received his *agrégation* in philosophy in 1927—one year after Herr's death—remarked how strangely personal this librarian's work was:

> "That a duty could be drained of its institutional anonymity to such a degree so as to become conflated with one of the strongest personalities we've seen: this is a moment in history that nothing can efface. In his library, Herr was not the administrator, he was the sovereign. He was not the curator—he was the creator!"[33]

A voracious curiosity

Even if Herr did not formalize his "documentary policy" for the library at the rue d'Ulm or leave behind any formalized documents about it, it is still possible to reconstitute how it functioned, and

---

32 Paul Vidal de la Bache, "La Bibliothèque de l'École," in *Le centenaire de l'ENS 1795–1895*, École Normale Supérieure, Paris, 1895, p. 447–53.

33 Georges Canguilhem, in *Bulletin de la société des amis de l'ENS*, no. 138, March 1977, p. 25.

what the major principles were. It was Herr himself who described his frenetic practice of reading and study as a "voracious curiosity."[34] He possessed incredible encyclopedic knowledge and Hubert Bourgin, who was ten years Herr's senior and among the original Dreyfusards, called him a "living encyclopedia." Not content with German, English, Latin and Greek, Herr learned Italian, several Slavic languages that included Russian, as well as a few Celtic languages: Welsh, Old Irish, and Breton. He knew these languages well enough to be able to write research articles about them and participate in contemporary philological debates that were extremely specialized.[35] He had countless disciplinary "specialties." He knew Hegelian philosophy just as well as Platonic. He had planned to write a bibliographical inventory of all the interpretations of Plato since the beginning and to make a systematic presentation of this colossal gloss. The book was to be called *Bibliotheca Platonica*. The Herr archives contain around 200 handwritten bibliographic records about the Platonic commentators of the Renaissance and the Reformation, and these undoubtedly constitute the beginnings of an overview of Platonic literature for this period.[36] His comparative commentaries on books, sometimes very long, attest more broadly to a great mastery of Rousseau, German idealism, English liberalism, economics in general, ancient philosophy, geography as it was emerging as its own discipline, and the political history of the European countries. The breadth of Herr's knowledge is truly incredible, and the overwhelming majority of testimonies about him communicate that Herr was astonishing in this respect.

This intellectual quality of being interested in everything was doubled by an impressive reading ability that he exhibited while a student at the ENS. Daniel Lindenberg and Pierre-André

---

34 See the important letter address to Andler on September 25, 1905, reproduced in Appendix 4.

35 See, for example, the article "De la transcription des noms slaves" in *Annales de géographie*, 1921, no. 166, reproduced in Lucien Herr, op. cit., p. 159–67.

36 Lucien Herr collection, Centre d'histoire de Sciences Po, LH5 D4.

Meyer have made a list of Herr's readings from the student loan records kept at the ENS library. The list of Herr's loans is so lengthy that it was necessary to add extra sheets for him in the huge ledgers. For the year 1885–1886, Herr borrowed, for the month of November: 106 items; December: 28; January: 18; February: 16; March: 10; April: 2; May: 58; June: 37; July: 12; August: 11. Herr's readings were essentially in German. Herr read Hegel, of course, as well his disciples (Feuerbach, Rosenkrantz), along with Fichte, Goethe, Schelling, Schlegel, Leibniz, and Kant. Works by German philosophers of the time were also in the library's collections and were among the items he borrowed (Schopenhauer, Duhring, Hartmann). The influence of positivism can be seen in the many works of Darwin (*Origin of Species*, *Descendancy of Man*) and John Stuart Mill that he took out on loan. Among the French philosophers, Herr was interested in the Enlightenment, especially Rousseau and Diderot, but also Condorcet. Nineteenth-century France is represented by Tocqueville, Comte, Renan, and Taine. Herr also borrowed works by Alfred Fouillée such as *La Science sociale contemporaine, Critique des systèmes de morale contemporains: Propriété sociale et démocratie*, and *L'Idée moderne de droit (Contemporary Social Science, Critique of Contemporary Moral Systems: Social Property and Democracy*, and *The Modern Notion of Law)* and Charles Renouvier's *Logique* and *Essais de critique (Logic* and *Critical Essays)*. These readings attest to an interest in the German sciences and for positivism, on the one hand, and the social sciences and humanities, on the other. Socialist works were not yet available at the ENS. Herr himself was the one to purchase Marx's *Das Kapital* (1867) in 1890.[37]

This extraordinary reading capacity was the primary tool of Herr's trade. An interesting testimony by Andler, who became even closer to Herr when they both entered "into socialism" in 1889, gives us a living portrait of the librarian at work. This testimony may be rather long, but the finesse of its analysis provides valuable, rare details about Herr's daily routine on the job:

---

37   Daniel Lindenberg and Pierre-André Meyer, op. cit., p. 211.

He loved his library. This is why he always remained attached to it. What was it like, this love to which he gave
his entire life? In the morning, when he would settle in
his big office, he would find the voluminous bundles of
foreign books in all different languages that the French
booksellers and warehousers had sent. He would open
them and make his top picks. Not a single book would
pass beneath his eyes without him scrutinizing it sum-
marily. He would subject the most important and the
most expensive to a thorough examination. This was always the case for new periodicals, the subscriptions to
which would incur annual expenses over the long term.
On other days, foreign doctoral dissertations would
pour in, hundreds at a time. They just needed to be classified, since under international trading conventions the
service was performed automatically at the ENS. Herr
went through them, took note of what might interest
anyone he knew working on a related subject. He reserved his thorough reading for books that were truly
innovative, those by scholars already of renown, and especially those by the future instructors. He had a "voracious curiosity" (the term was his) for these intellectual
novelties in all matters. There is no need to hide the fact
that he had the imperious need to be the the first and often the only one to know, to be unbeatable in all the records for rapid and immediate information in all the disciplines that mattered. He did not tolerate anyone else
knowing more than him, before him. We do not dispute
this advantage or glory. We benefited far too much from
his ambitions. We found all the excellent books sorted
while we were still looking for them in the weekly or annual catalogs, or in the bibliographies of the journals.
His art of reading quickly and discerningly, and of re-
taining everything with such precision, defies any comparison. In his early years, Herr's memory was prodi-
gous. It was in this way that he came to know his library
from within, like none of his predecessors did. He could

> not only tell you what volumes he had in each discipline,
> but the chapters of the volumes and the articles of the
> journals. When newcomers arrived he would lead them
> straight to the shelf where they were sure to find the in-
> formation they were looking for.[38]

In this passage we find the primary elements that constituted Herr's method for acquisitions, which was connected to his practice of reading quickly, prodigously, and critically. The result, it seems, was an exercise of acquisitions that remained solitary. According to Andler, Herr worked directly with books from his office at the library. The sources are missing to determine if he used professional tools such as publishers' catalogs or book reviews. Additionally, it is not known if he accounted for the collections at neighboring libraries such as the Sorbonne's for the sake of complementarity. In any case, what is certain and consistent with what is already known about him is that Herr was constantly on the lookout for innovative publications, obsessed with detecting any advances in knowledge as soon as possible so as to be able to track their progress.

The Library's Readers

But Herr appeared first and foremost to be focused on the patrons of the library. The notes he took while reading prove that bibliographical advice—in short, orienting readers—was at the heart of his vision for the profession of librarian. Works were sorted and selected not just according to their intrinsic qualities, but also according to possible readings and the uses that he anticipated students having for them. It was a vision that was utilitarian, not in the pejorative sense but rather in the sense of the intellectual and social utility that these books could offer. Excellent knowledge of the student body made it possible for Herr to make such assessments. Andler recalls that Herr was closer to the students than the instructors were. Emile Gau, who had attended the ENS and who became

---

38   Charles Andler. op. cit., p. 105–106.

the general director of public instruction and fine arts in Tunisia in 1930, recalls:

> He would leave his library a little before noon and come to the "Archicubes" refectory to take his place at the spot reserved for him, which was the little end of the long table, and from where he saw everyone. I think that he could relax there; he truly experienced our lives as young people, was interested in everything, what we did for fun as well as our work, guiding us in our research, telling us about publications and simultaneously finding out about their content from us. Later he told me that he found himself benefiting from this ongoing contact with "the young people" who were all working on original research.[39]

Hubert Bourgin echoes this sentiment when he describes how Herr would dispense his advice:

> This man would interrogate you with his pressing but reserved curiosity, with a clear and decisive discretion that seemed divinatory—he knew everything about a total discipline, with each of his words summarizing the bibliographies, the references, and the index cards, expressing overwhelming knowledge that did away with uncertainties, indecision, and clumsy trial-and-error. He knew the sciences from all the books as well as those that were gestating in the minds of all his contemporaries. No matter what it was you were doing, whatever work you'd undertaken, he knew the ins and outs.[40]

---

39 Letter dated December 29, 1930 from Emile Gau à Mme Lucien Herr, LH8 dossier 1.

40 Hubert Bourgin, *De Jaurès à Léon Blum, l'Ecole normale et la politique*, Fayard, Paris, 1938, p. 109.

The excellent knowledge that Herr appeared to have both of his readers and his resources made it possible to provide informed advice that was, in more contemporary terms, "personalized," making the librarian the essential, central point of contact for any work of research. Though Herr would lead newcomers "right to the shelf where they were certain to find the information they were looking for," he also encouraged free access to works. He gave students "the right to wander amidst the stacks, to explore the resources volume by volume, to experience the books themselves."[41]

The records of his archival resources are brimming with notes bearing the library letterhead, addressed to students as well as professors and friends, dispensing bibliographical advice. In 1899, he wrote to Célestin Bouglé, who was preparing a study on the caste regime (which was not published until 1908):[42]

> My dear friend, a word to draw your attention to a new book by the Jesuit Joseph Dahlmann, who is, as you know, a specialist in India, especially the *Mahabharata*. It's called *Das altindische Volkstum und seine Bedeutung für die Gesellschaftskunde*, Köln, Bachen, 2.25 marks (140 pp. In 8°). The book is not, I believe, very new, but it's all about castes and guilds, and since he knows the literature of the subject well, he may of use to you. I'll bring it in for you just in case. If, after examination, it does not tell you anything, you can return it to me and I will keep it for myself.[43]

And, several months later:

> My dear friend, I will have your pieces of information, at least one of which is difficult to find with my own

---

41   Charles Andler, op. cit., p. 106.

42   Célestin Bougle, *Essai sur le régime des castes*, Paris, Alcan, 1908.

43   Letter of 1899 from Lucien Herr to Célestin Bouglé, LH3 dossier 4.

> resources, since the book was published in Calcutta or
> Bombay... I'll look again. I'm sincere, these aren't just
> words; I beg of you, make use of us (I mean our good
> bibliographic will).[44]

Herr considered this particularly attentive and precise documentary attention to be an integral part of his job as a librarian. His public, or his "clientele," as he curiously referred to the readers at the library and, later, the pedagogical museum, formed a circle around him that he served as best as possible, in various ways. Hubert Bourgin described the librarian amidst his readers in the following way:

> His eruptions of joy, his sudden bursts of Homeric laugh-
> ter, would shake him and bring him to tears, his rages
> of impatience resounding with curses would make the
> cages rattle, and they would surprise the previously un-
> initiated readers near and far. But the initiated were nu-
> merous: students, former students of all ages, professors,
> scholars, foreigners from many different countries.[45]

This lively testimony of the circles of regulars that had formed at the library is characteristic of the affectionate qualities of so many descriptions of the librarian. The written portrayals of Herr as a mustachioed, booming giant often contain such quixotic, epic terms that he sometimes seems to be a character from a tale about Parisian intellectual life of the early twentieth century. This legendary dimension of the "Herrian literature" makes it possible to get an idea of the real and profound fascination that he has elicited since his time at the library, where he left such a personal imprint.

---

44   Letter dated February 12, 1900 from Lucien Herr to Célestin Bouglé, LH3
      dossier 4.

45   Hubert Bourgin, op. cit., p. 109.

Additions to the library

The credits granted to the library were, as we shall see below, too limited to permit Herr to fulfill his ambitions. Part of his activity therefore consisted of complementing his costly acquisitions with various procurements, determined by what he was doing outside the library. Constant additions were already provided by the Ministère de l'Instruction publique (Ministry of Public Instruction). Based on an arrangement from 1882, the ministry provided the library with university publications from abroad, which it received in exchange for French doctoral dissertations. In addition, the different ministries for public works, commerce, agriculture, the interior, finance, foreign affairs, colonies, the city of Paris, and the prefecture of the Seine all graciously sent him their primary publications.[46] Andler further notes:

> Herr knew like nobody else how to direct gifts of all kinds to the library. Families of deceased academics often allowed him to choose the most valuable books from their libraries. Many gave him their rare volumes while they were still alive. How many volumes from his own library, purchased once at a great price, did Herr himself donate?[47]

The library received from one Monsieur Lerambert, a professor of English who died in 1890, a collection of 3000 volumes of history, geography, political economics, and foreign literatures.[48] However, we do not know if this gift is directly attributable to Herr. Three years before, the library had received, under Monsieur Rébelliau's direction, another significant donation from an instructor at the ENS. On the other hand, his collaboration with journals,

---

46   Paul Vidal de la Bache, op. cit., p. 451.

47   Charles Andler, op. cit., p. 107–108.

48   Paul Vidal de la Bache, op. cit., p. 448.

particularly the *Revue critique d'histoire et de littérature* (*Critical Review of History and Literature*) of the Germanist at the ENS, Arthur Chuquet, allowed him to gather important resources. He worked at the journal from 1888 to 1893, and over this five-year period he made an arrangement with Chuquet for the *Revue* to give the ENS all the German journals it received. However, after Chuquet was appointed to the Collège de France in 1893, he left the ENS at the request of the director Georges Perrot and then stopped making donations to the library. Herr himself left the journal and harbored a long resentment towards Chuquet. He revisited the matter almost ten years later in his report of 1902:

> We mustn't forget an incident that had rather difficult consequences for the library, the departure of Monsieur Chuquet. When he left, he retracted the free usage of periodicals, the annual subscription price for which was at least a thousand francs. More than half were of considerable importance and were now being charged to our budget.[49]

However, collaborating with journals also often allowed him to receive the books that he reviewed. In addition, for the many editorial suggestions he gave to authors, he often received compensation in the form of gifts, which he would accept without hesitation. The correspondence between Herr and Xavier Léon, who at the time was grappling with his work on Fichte[50], attests to this: "I'm sure you already considered sending a copy to the library of the Ecole, and I thank you in advance. You know that I beg shamelessly for my poor library."[51]

---

49 Report dated October 25, 1902 from Lucien Herr to the director of the Ecole about the library's financial situation. This document is reproduced in its entirety in Appendix 3. It is located in the French national archives under 61 AP/157.

50 Xavier Leon, *Fichte et son temps*, published between 1922 and 1927, Armand Colin, Paris.

51 Undated letter from Lucien Herr to Xavier Leon, LH3 dossier 2.

The library's acquisition records also attest to the purchase of used materials, which though infrequent deserves mention. Unfortunately, there is not very much information that would make it possible to determine where these below market-priced works were purchased. In early 1914, the war interrupted relations with German publishers, even for annual subscriptions to certain periodicals paid in advance. This interruption lasted for six years and completely disrupted the organization of the library's collection.

After the war, the Direction de l'Enseignement Supérieur (Directorate of Higher Education) assigned Herr to reconnect with German publishers to catch up on the huge backlog of collections and to conduct negotiations for all libraries in France. The Directorate chose Herr because of his good relationships with and knowledge of the German intelligentsia. A letter from the Minister of Public Instruction dated December 6, 1921, thanked Herr for his efforts regarding two railway cars full of books sent by Germany in reparation.[52] Unfortunately, we do not know the details of these transactions and Andler himself relates the episode rather quickly.[53] However, this is a testament to Herr's pacifism and his efforts to promote intellectual exchange and to revive cooperation between France and Germany following the war.

Encouraging New Thought

A research library

In his report dated 1902, Herr set out his goals for the ENS library. These were to serve him as the bases for its development and communicated a dual function for the library: it was to be a place of learning as well as research. The opening of new sections taught at the ENS led to considerable development of the library, which was compelled to create new resources from scratch.

----

52   These documents are located in carton LH2 dossier 3.

53   Charles Andler, op. cit., p. 312.

> I only want to recall the creations and innovations that made the constitution or the rapid, almost immediate growth of categories of books which scarcely existed, or were very badly represented, so essential. First, there were the arrangements at the Ecole for the instruction and study of natural sciences, which burdened the budget with the need to make a considerable number of expensive subscriptions. It was then the creation of the living language sections, which, quite deprived of work instruments at the outset, had to be equipped very quickly, taking advantage of opportunities to fill gaps that were too severe by immediately constituting the first indispensable stock of classic texts and course books, etc. There was then the very rapid development of contemporary history studies, which necessitated the speedy acquisition of a fairly large number of books that were completely missing from the library. There was the continuous development of geographic studies, which required the expensive enrichment of a section that was very poorly represented when I was called to the library.[54]

The ENS was finally taking a turn towards modernity, giving burgeoning disciplines their rightful place. Herr himself was a strong supporter of the new social sciences, and he gave them particular priority in his budget. But the library was also to be a research library that met the conditions needed for the generation of new ideas. Thus:

> I considered this library as a living organism that needed to be methodically developed and enriched. I always thought it had to guide, illuminate, and invite research rather than just support it. All the new directions in students' work, the expansion of their scientific curiosity, the works of history—especially contemporary

---

54   Report of 1902, see Appendix 3.

history—of philosophy, geography, and sociology, that are now the pride of the École would have been impossible undertakings even with the resources that our library had fifteen years ago, and in this I find some acknowledgment and reward for my efforts.[55]

"Guide, illuminate, invite": the Herrian library was active, not just a repository of knowledge stored in books. On the contrary, it was a place where the librarian, who knew the collections and what they contained, could bring them to life so as to prompt dialogues, foster questions, and indicate which directions to follow. The librarian was the mediator who created points of access between readers and books, allowing for the dissemination of knowledge. The method that presided over the creation of collections was based first and foremost upon the requirement for constant updates. In this way, the library would remain current in all fields, particularly the new disciplines that were changing the character of scholarship in France, and likewise give more and more room to social sciences. Periodicals occupied a pride of place. There was also an enlightened choice of scholarly production: the idea was not to have everything, nor was it, as Vidal de la Blache described above, to privilege special erudition and monographs about very specialized subjects. As Herr envisioned it, the library was to be more of a catalyst to young researchers' curiosity.

> I did not proceed as a bibliophile or a maniacal collector but I took every care so that the primary, essential instruments were available there for all works, today more differentiated and more varied than ever, that anyone undertook at the École. I knew it would always be impossible to complete a special scholarly work with our resources alone, but I thought that it should be possible to undertake and begin all works with our resources.

---

55 Report of 1902.

The composition of the collections would have to support this *tour de force* of offering an extensive representation of knowledge by maintaining complementarity among resources ("all works"). It is striking that Herr often used terms like "instruments" and "tools" (*instruments, outils*): the librarian was the one who worked with this raw material and who made it available for use.

The Citadel of Dreyfusism

Herr was a socialist starting in 1888. A vast political awareness was to organize around him and his library. He had great influence on the young Normaliens, who often came from the *républican* bourgeoisie and would have tended to turn to someone like Clemenceau. At the library of the ENS, they encountered an intellectual of an entirely new kind, an unprecedented character for whom socialism, scholarship, and disinterestedness were inextricably linked. He had a kind of purity of mind, turning away from a path of ambition so as to choose a career without glory in order to devote himself to the community.

Accounts by those who were at the ENS while Herr worked there agree that Herr started to have an effective influence with the class of 1892. Before the start of the Dreyfusard battle, Herr was the mentor[56] to a small group of socialist Normaliens. From this date onwards, the number of students who came to socialism through his actions multiplied. We owe him two historical "conversions": Jaurès and Blum. This trio enjoys a particular prestige and was a considerable source of firepower during the Dreyfus Affair.

It was at the ENS library that Herr met Jean Jaurès at the end of 1889, when the latter had just been defeated in the Tarn elections. He was taking advantage of this forced pause in his political career to resume the preparation of his doctoral dissertations. He came to the library to stock up on books. The influence that Herr had on his conversion from *républicainisme* to socialism has been established. For two years, Jaurès assiduously frequented the library

---

56   Daniel Lindenberg and Pierre-André Meyer, op. cit., p. 138.

and was in frequent contact with Herr, who was five years his junior. In his *Souvenirs sur l'Affaire (Memories of the Dreyfus Affair)*, Blum wrote that rather than speak of a "conversion" to socialism that Herr brought about in Jaurès, it was more accurate to say that Herr helped him rather to realize that he was a socialist.[57]

Léon Blum also met Herr at the ENS library. A famous anecdote relates that one day in 1893, the two men met by chance at the Place de la Concorde. Blum recounted this episode, where Herr acted as a mentor helping to elicit his friend's socialist inclinations:

> One day, in 1893, I met him at the Place de la Concorde. He was going to the *Revue de Paris*. We walked for two hours along the Champs-Elysées. Our friendship became close. It was Herr, already involved in the socialist world and registered with the Allemanists, who crystallized all the diffuse tendencies in me and effected the shift from my individualistic and anarchist spirit towards socialism.[58]

Herr would visit Blum daily, biking to his vacation house in the Parisian area. By September 1897, Blum knew that Dreyfus was innocent, and this was because of Herr. His analysis of Herr's influence refutes the notion that he proselytized or was intellectually dominating, evoking instead a power of entirely methodical conviction that respected the freedom of his interlocutors:

> Herr's strength—an incredible strength that is truly unique, insofar as I've never observed it to the same degree in anybody else—was essentially due to this: in him, conviction assumed the form of evidence. He understood the truth with a power that was so complete and calm that he communicated it effortlessly and

---

57   Léon Blum, *Souvenirs sur l'Affaire*, Gallimard, Paris, 1935, p. 28.

58   Louis Lévy, *Comment ils sont devenus socialistes*, cited by Daniel Lindenberg, op. cit., p. 138.

directly. He emanated this assurance with all his being: "Yes, I think this, I believe that," and we realized that indeed, we thought and we believed as he did; we even had the impression, or the illusion, of always having secretly harbored that same thought, or that belief. We no longer knew if he had persuaded you or revealed what you actually were to yourself... Such was the man who had affirmed to me, out of the blue as we were walking down a garden path, "Dreyfus is innocent" and who, seeing me captured and already nearly convinced by his voice, then told me the facts one after the other, the arguments and the evidence.[59]

Until then, most of the Dreyfusards "of the first hour" did not really take the revelations of Bernard Lazare seriously. A writer who was a friend of the Dreyfus family, Lazare had published a sensational article entitled "Une erreur judiciaire. La vérité sur l'Affaire Dreyfus" ("A Miscarriage of Justice. The Truth about the Dreyfus Affair). Thanks to his friendship with the former Normalien Lucien Lévy-Bruhl, who was also the Captain's cousin, Herr had early access to key elements of the case. At the end of 1897, when the case had still not yet been brought before the public, he was the one who had the idea of launching a petition for intellectuals who were in favor of a retrial. It is moving to find among his papers the first version of the "list of intellectuals to be contacted"[60] because they were liable to sign.

Herr helped to position the ENS at the forefront of the Dreyfus battle through his mobilization of professors and pupils alike, who were among the earliest signatories to be recruited: Gabriel Monod, the positivist historian, was one of the first to support the cause; Jules Tannery, who was the assistant director of the ENS (Science Section); the professor of German Charles Andler;

---

59 Léon Blum, op. cit., p. 519.

60 This list is in carton LH2 dossier 1.

the history professor Gustave Bloch; and Gustave Lanson, who was a deputy for Ferdinand Brunetière and the future director of the ENS. Of the students, Herr's most important recruit was Peguy, who led Herr to his young peers such as François Simiand as well as Célestin Bouglé and Maurice Halbwachs, who were won over particularly through Durkheim's efforts. Among the youngest were Mario Roques, Désiré Roustan, Paul Langevin, and Hubert Bourgin, who finished their courses at the start of the Affair.

When Barrès wrote a text for *L'Echo de Paris*, the text that mocked the intellectuals' manifesto in the *Revue Blanche*, it was Herr who answered him on behalf of those who had signed the protest. His article, "A Maurice Barrès" ("To Maurice Barrès"), appeared in the journal on February 15, 1898. Herr wrote, "I am one of those 'intellectuals' whose protest has so greatly amused you."[61] It is not our purpose here to recount the rest of the Dreyfus Affair, which was now underway. It suffices to say that this period was a pivotal one for the entire history of ideas and the social history of France and the library was, thanks to Herr, the central point where the new class of intellectuals invented itself.

Socialist Recruiter?

In works about Herr, there are two opposing interpretations of the political dimensions of his position as ENS librarian. Did his commitment as a librarian have a strategic element? All would answer in the affirmative. Was Herr a recruiter for socialism? This matter is a thornier one.

Until 1898–1899, socialism and Dreyfusism did not overlap. The leading figures of parliamentary socialism such as Jaurès and Millerand and the socialist leaders like Guesde and Vaillant saw no need to involve the proletariat in the Affair. In addition, the majority of accounts agree that Herr only opened up about his socialist ideas after being sure of his interlocutors' convictions. Hubert Bourgin, a former friend and a disappointed socialist who had

---

61   Text reproduced in Lucien Herr, *Choix d'écrits 1, Politique*, Rieder, Paris, 1932, p. 39.

passed on to nationalism, supported the theory that Herr was a recruiter for the socialist cause. In his book, *L'Ecole normale et la politique* (*The Ecole Normale and Politics*), he explained how difficult it was for the students of the "Herr years" to resist the influence of the combined teachings of Herr and Andler, and not become socialists. He did not attribute the many "conversions" to active propagandizing on the part of the two friends, but rather to a "magnetism of a magnitude of which they were aware" and to a deliberately complementary organization of talks. Thus, "how could we have escaped the implicit conclusion of all this instruction? Everything fit together, everything was admitted and became incorporated into our thought ... The magician [Andler] completed the work of the Titan of the library."[62] Thus, "Herr's actions were extended outside by those of a growing number of young men whom he had made socialists."[63]

Bourgin's text about Herr, which he wrote three decades after the Affair at the age of just over 60, is both surprising and paradoxical. If he supports the theory of a certain indoctrination of the minds of the ENS, he was also a contemporary of Herr's who left behind the most interesting and detailed pages about the librarian. Perhaps Bourgin's mistrust, in his later years, of the legendary librarian was in direct proportion to his previous admiration. Perhaps there are also, as Lindenberg and Meyer suggest, other unpleasant reasons associated with the political climate of 1938, when *L'Ecole normale et la politique* was published.[64]

It is useless to attempt to settle the debate from sources that are primarily second-hand, though it is possible to detect patterns in such sources. In the article previously cited by Robert John Smith, the author states that "the librarian's influence was more cultural than political. He was rather a scholar who gave himself to developing the library and advising other young scholars. The

---

62   Hubert Bourgin, op. cit., p. 140.

63   Hubert Bourgin, op. cit., p. 105.

64   Daniel Lindenberg, op. cit., p. 59.

students who rejected his political opinions still sought and appreciated his academic advice because his erudition, his devotion, and his rectitude were respected."[65]

There are many accounts that corroborate this interpretation. Raoul Blanchard, a geographer who had studied under Vidal de la Blache from 1897, a friend of Peguy's but hardly a socialist, states:

> I can only envision him in his library, sitting behind a high counter where the books and the catalogs were piled up, his immense forehead and long face already incised with vigorous wrinkles, a rather harsh appearance that worried the newcomers, but his courtesy, let's say his generosity, was revealed quickly through his abrupt manners. It was important for him to inform the poor boys who didn't know because he, Lucien Herr, knew, and his erudition was immense. This courtesy, this knowledge, all the way up to his demeanor, earned him our sympathies: he was very popular among us … We loved him and he loved us; but we did not follow him.[66]

Ernest Tonnelat (1877–1948), a Germanist and historian who had attended the ENS, recruited by Péguy at the time of the Affair, wrote in 1928:

> I was struck from the beginning to see with what reserve he would conduct thoughts and souls. Many times after that I heard or read that Herr had practiced some sort of youth recruitment, that he had indoctrinated them, that he was a kind of occult leader. I remembered the discretion, the true intellectual respect

65   Robert John Smith, "L'atmosphère politique à l'ENS à la fin du 19ème siècle," *Revue d'histoire moderne et contemporaine*, April-June 1973, no. 20, p. 251.

66   Raoul Blanchard, *Sous l'aile de Péguy*, Paris: Arthème Fayard, 1961, p. 191.

he had always had for those of our classmates who, like me, would approach him shyly. To accuse him of trying to dominate was true slander. You'd go to him spontaneously, as to an invigorating wellspring. If anyone at that time was concerned with recruitment, it was Peguy. Herr let himself be approached, but seemed to make it a point of honor to not exert on anyone anything that resembled a moral constraint ... I saw in Lucien Herr a gifted master with a great virtue: that of teaching people to be themselves."[67]

Andler recounted that Herr only shared his socialist convictions with him after Andler had declared himself. It is possible to question this account, however, in two ways: first of all because it comes from a friend who sought to pay tribute to a great man unjustly forgotten, and also because it comes from a socialist, himself involved in disseminating these ideas at the ENS. However, Andler explains at considerable length the moral dilemma that confronted both him and Herr in terms of how compatible the neutrality obligation associated with their official status was with their political commitment.[68] "We thought that outside of service, we had the right to profess the political and social opinions we believed to be true," he explains. It is also in the interests of discretion and compartmentalization between these two activities that Herr wrote in the *Parti ouvrier* (*Workers Party*), a mouthpiece of the POSR (*Parti Ouvrier Socialiste Révolutionnaire*, Revolutionary Socialist Workers Party), under the pseudonym of Pierre Breton.

Finally, it is important to note that Herr's correspondence with young people who asked him for advice is a testament to his good faith and neutrality. Responding to a girl in his family who sought his advice about her political commitment, Herr wrote with great warmth and kindness:

---

67   Letter dated October 1928 from Ernest Tonnelat to Charles Andler, LH3 dossier 6.

68   Herr, p. 119.

> In these matters, one does not dictate a solution and a
> ready-made formula to another person. I have already
> told you that nobody has the right to impinge on you,
> to use an upper hand, age, or external authority, to ex-
> ert on you a pressure or a direction. It is necessary that
> within you, matters be ordered and clarified by your
> own efforts.[69]

In this striking manner, Herr shows a young mind the path of criticism and freedom that are at the very foundation of his thought.

If Herr devoted a large part of his life to socialist action, the
strategic scope from his place at the rue d'Ulm was broader than
mere partisan commitment. In other terms, it was the overall conception that Herr had of collective progress that included socialism
rather than the opposite. Socialism was seen as a possible concrete
realization of this ideal. But the concept of liberation did not just
concern the proletariat. It was the force underlying a more essential notion of history.

Management Difficulties

Recurring deficits

Herr asserted himself as master of his library. This was not, however, without its challenges. The three main documents that make it
possible to grasp the conception that Herr had of his role at the library are available in the appendix. The first is a report dated November 22, 1890, addressed to the director of the ENS, and mentions serious financial difficulties for the library. The second report
is from twelve years later, dated October 15, 1902, and still insists
on the poverty of resources. These two letters have a distinct tone
of justification. Andler explains it as Herr's rather "autocratic" exercise of the directorial role, which is perhaps the necessary counterpart of one who knows how to handle so well "the librarian's art of

---

69   Letter of February 19, 1915, cited by Andler, p. 340.

the timely purchase," but which led to so many calls to order from the ministry offices.[70]

The report of 1890 is one of the first that Herr wrote. Appointed as librarian in August 1888, he gradually discovered how the credits attributed to him worked. At the end of the year, a variable amount from the balance of the ENS's general budget was added to a fixed budget of about 8,000 francs. For around ten years, the library's annual expenditures had been equal, or more often than not, equal to 12,000 francs. For his first year in 1888, Herr indicated that he had been able to respect this average: with a debit of 12,000 francs, he had been able to handle his expenses.

In his second year as librarian, Herr had to confront a deficit that he did not know how to manage: the decrease in the complementary credit, which was not compensated for by an increase in the fixed allocation, threatened the accounts for the years to come. His efforts at economizing, at what Herr called "miserliness," first affected the physical treatment intended for the preservation of documents, particularly binding. Herr's priority was to dedicate the most money to purchases. Herr called on Directeur Perrot's generosity to increase the allowance for the library. This additional credit was a major problem: its allocation at the end of the year did not correspond to the natural rhythm of acquisitions in the library, which for someone like Herr, so attuned to the newest developments, was based on schedules for the publication of monographs; subscriptions, often honored on a one-time basis at the start or end of the year; and serial works that would account for a share of the funds from year to year. The librarian had little room for maneuver and refused to sacrifice recent acquisitions, which constituted precisely the heart of the documentary policy he had established for himself.

The 1902 report was even more urgent. During these twelve years and despite repeated requests from Herr, the library did not get any additional credits. The fixed allocation remained around 8,000 francs, and the extraordinary credit continued to decline.

---

70   Charles Andler, op. cit., p. 107.

The library was then in an alarming state: the deficit increased enormously, reaching around 12,000 francs; this had been a strategic choice for Herr, who preferred to spread the debt from the new collections, created from scratch, over several years so as not to immobilize the library's budget for this purpose alone. It remains that successive deferrals of deficits to the next year, together with the fees consecrated to the new collections that Herr prioritized, would require an increase in resources. But the credits, on the contrary, tended to be diminished.

Reading these reports tells us that Herr was the opposite of a manager in the contemporary sense of the term. Though he may have maintained his accounts scrupulously, the prevailing logic was not to balance resources, but to be attentive to intellectual output. Herr was first of all a scholar who could simply not refrain from purchasing, and could not even delay purchasing, certain titles deemed indispensable, such as "the three volumes of the Greek and Latin corpus, and several expensive volumes of *Monuments Germanica historica*." Likewise, "it is impossible to predict a fixed date for the publication of the very expensive volumes of the *Faune du Golfe de Naples* (*Fauna of the Gulf of Naples*), or *Monuments antichi* (*Antichi Monuments*)."[71] The consequence of this logic was that it was inevitable that the funds for books would be exceeded on a regular basis. The interests of a well-organized library reigned, and Herr's orders for the library were very deliberate:

> I know, and I knew it would have been more prudent
> on my part to have taken no initiative, to have made the
> purchases required by the faculty within the limits of
> the budgetary resources, and stopped there. If I proceed-
> ed otherwise, it was deliberately, out of the passionate
> dedication to the work that has been entrusted to me.[72]

---

71   Report of 1902.

72   Report of 1902.

It appears that such choices did not always make Herr particularly popular. "I have fortified myself against recriminations and insults, of which there is no shortage, as you know,"[73] he wrote to Georges Perrot in 1890. Twelve years later, also writing to Perrot, he explained, "I did not blindly surrender to requests from teachers or students."[74] Did he ignore these suggestions for purchase and bibliographies for courses, or merely disregard them? There are not enough details to confirm this, but these statements, as well as a tactful yet irritated report from Andler, reveal the bibliographic authoritarianism that Herr exerted over his library. Andler conceded that "He also—let us not hide this character trait—had the imperious need to be the first, and often the only one to know, to be unbeatable in all records of fast, immediate information, in any discipline that mattered. He did not tolerate anyone else knowing more than he did, before he did." A memory of Bourgin's describes the moral and authoritarian influence that Herr cultivated in this temple of knowledge:

> There are fields he condemns and that he despises: to confess that we have ventured there and we like it is to confess to being a fool. There are recommended and sacred fields; there is philosophy, sociology, German studies, special areas of scholarship; but you must be worthy of entering them. And if one claims to believe to possess this worth, what trials this exposes one to! Lucien Herr was a judge of men as well as of things, their current and potential abilities as works done and to do. A universal judge, a universally competent judge. But a biased and passionate judge. We know, we say that he was fierce, that he had—not for personal reasons, as he was perfectly selfless, but scientific and political ones—great anger, not raging, because he was master of himself and

---

73   Report of 1890

74   Report of 1902.

mastered all situations, but gigantic like him and like his erudition … Whoever rubs him the wrong way, beware![75]

Two recurring models

One final document is an undated draft of a letter for an unknown recipient. This document communicates a vehement protest against the Bibliothèque Nationale's acquisition methods and provides a useful counterpoint to better grasp the principles governing Herr's activity.[76] Herr rebelled violently against the imbalance of resources between research libraries and the Bibliothèque Nationale and the latter's whimsical purchasing methods, in particular with regard to German books (a field which did not figure as part of legal deposit). In this respect, the Bibliothèque Nationale seemed to exhibit great nonchalance coupled with an almost complete lack of knowledge in the selection of its purchases.

> The scandal *par excellence* is the Bibliothèque Nationale. For more than thirty years, I have browsed its list of acquisitions with amazement. I did not have a precise image of its wealth, nor of the absurdity of this wealth, nor the incredible severity of its deficiencies …. It is haunted by the idea—chimerical, but reasonable up to a point with respect to French production—that the ideal would be to have everything. Since it cannot have everything, it takes at least a little bit of everything, as much as possible, without critique, without the least concern for utility or the needs for research and study, and then, once its credits are spent, it stops, waits for the following year, and starts again …. Of the 1,500 German periodicals it receives, I am absolutely certain that at least 1000 do not have a single reader in a given year. And, because it

---

75   Hubert Bourgin, op. cit., p. 109–10.

76   This letter is in the collection of the Sciences Po, LH1 dossier 6. The text is reproduced in Appendix 4.

> is easier to continue what one has started and librarians rarely resign themselves to interrupting a series, it follows that they continue to calmly receive a mass of obsolete periodicals, and there is not a penny left for young, energetic periodicals. As for purchases of new books, the mediocre portion of the credit devoted to it seems to be spent randomly, at the whim of what happens to be offered, or at the request of I do not know what maniacs who are curious about bizarre singularities.

The attack is a lively one. Justified or not, it certainly makes it possible to clearly establish two opposing models of librarianship in Herr's mind: a poorly grasped practice of patrimony, driven by an illusory exhaustiveness based on a practice of taking "a little of everything" and, most importantly, "without critique, without the least concern for utility" versus a policy of severe selection oriented towards contemporary matters.

This drastic selection was essential, for the ENS at any rate, for financial reasons. Herr had to sharpen his vision in order to only purchase what was best. But it was also a fundamental element for the composition of a quality library, and above all, that was oriented towards those who used it. The important thing for Herr was to make his library alive—that is, usable and accessible.

The Librarian's Tragedy

Choice was a matter at the heart of Herr's practice as a librarian. This involved refusing to honor requests from professors and continuing to maintain subscriptions, as well as forging discriminating criteria for deciding what to keep and what to reject from a collection of 100,000 books managed alone with a *garçon de bibliothèque*. It is possible to see how the librarian's profession can assume the form of an imperious vocation requiring constant investment and stubborn commitment. In the 1902 report, Herr wrote, "I have done what I could to put myself in a position to appreciate the necessary work instruments." This meant becoming a specialist in everything so as to be the legitimate judge of what was good and what was not.

This could only be the colossal and insane project of a life-time. And in fact, a superb and poignant letter written to Andler in 1905[77] reveals the librarian's tragedy: torn between the call of research and scholarship, on the one hand, and self-sacrifice in the service of the community, on the other, Herr pushed his own learning in his service to others, but without ever setting anything down, without ever producing anything original—that is, without ever writing anything. It has been mentioned how much Andler regretted this. It seems that in some moments of doubt, Herr also regretted that his loyalty to the cause of the collective mind made him a failure. This is clear from a letter Herr wrote attempting to persuade Andler to publish his lecture notes:

> It is absolutely necessary that you make available to a general public this tremendous work of guidance and understanding that is not made just for your students … This is what distresses me the most, in my *vie manquée*. I know the services that I have provided, and I do not need to be comforted; but I also know everything that I have really learned, known, and understood—at least in my own way—of things, and how absurd it is that the community cannot take advantage of these long years of work, and that others will have to do them again. What would my life be like, if I were to reorganize it—and would it leave me the leisure and the desire to get a hold of the things I have known, one by one, and push them further and set them down, and would I be able to extract something that is communicable and that is worth being communicated? I do not know, and I doubt it. (…)
>
> For each subject, big or small, that I've touched, each time I've seen myself led to push my study as far as possible, out of an irresistible need and voracious curiosity, to not content myself with preconceptions, to get the

---

77   Letter dated from September 25, 1905 from Lucien Herr to Charles Andler, reproduced in Antoinette Blum, op. cit., lettre 10. This letter, which expresses the "librarian condition" with great precision and emotion, is reproduced in Appendix 5.

documents back in my hands and do the critical work again. I have, on the way, found quite a few points (particularly in patristics, religious history, in Celtic studies), things that have since been discovered by others, for my own pleasure; but I never cared much. I had various specialties, but I was never an expert, and I always considered myself satisfied when I understood (or believed I understood) the whole or the detail that had given me pause or seduced me (…)

You know all this as well as I do. This is true even of the two big subjects that I dreamed of devoting my life to, twenty years ago—the history of Hegelianism and the history of Platonism. What will I find when I really stir all the ashes that were extinguished so long ago and forgotten? Without a doubt, very little.–And then, my mind and my heart are gone, I am no longer interested in things that are purely speculative. I am only capable of passionate interest in what leads to practice, to intellectual and social development.

This lengthy quote demonstrates the magnitude of this renunciation. Even while encouraging his friend to write down his own works, he reaffirms his faithfulness to "intellectual and social development," to the common good. The tone is so passionate, even when it comes to lamenting his "vie manquée," echoing the feverish application letter he had sent to Perrot 18 years earlier. Does this letter express bitter regret at having sacrificed a potentially brilliant career for a position that forced him to work for others? The lamentation was rather at not having been able to advance knowledge enough or to benefit the community with his accumulated understanding, now lost and smothered by the weight of a hundred new readings, by committing all his discoveries to print.

The librarian Herr approached uncharted territories, then passed the baton: he was a ferryman between ideas and the world, officiating from amidst his library's walls of books. In his book, *L'Ecole normale et la politique* (*The Ecole Normale and Politics*), Bourgin calls Herr the "librarian consultant bibliographer" of the rue d'Ulm.[78] This playful name accurately sums up the form that Herr gave to his role as librarian, enriched by complementary activities that assume their full meaning as they converge in the bright foyer of the library. The bibliographic vocation expressed in the reviews that Herr wrote for the *Revue critique d'histoire et de littérature* (*Critical Review of History and Literature*) and the *Revue universitaire* (*University Review*) for six years was in some ways the formalized version of such a practice. The bibliography transforms the secular vision of ordinary librarianship—enriching the collections based on recommendations from professors—and endows librarians with full legitimacy to constitute the ideal library themselves. The book review provided the model of a practice that organized the description of the content of new publications and encouraged the emergence of new thinking.

Herr's Critics

Definition of the Corpus

From April 1888 to May 1893, Herr collaborated with several journals. In April 1888, Arthur Chuquet, the Germanist of the rue d'Ulm, recruited him to contribute literary reviews to his *Revue critique d'histoire et de littérature* (*Critical Review of History and Literature*). Herr left the journal five years later in May 1893 after having a sharp disagreement with Chuquet. Starting in January 1893, Herr was in charge of a section similar to the *Revue universitaire*, founded by the Normalien and Docteur ès lettres Paul Crouzet. Herr's work there lasted until July 1894. Meanwhile, Ernest Lavisse recruited him on January 1, 1894, this time as editorial secretary, for the *Revue de Paris*. There are no articles in this journal, where Herr would remain for ten years until January 30, 1904, that bear Herr's signature.

Herr's journalistic activity[79] was not limited to these scholarly research journals. He was also very active as a political journalist.

---

78   Bourgin, op. cit., p. 137.

79   On this subject, see the article of Simone Fraisse, "Lucien Herr, journaliste 1888–1905," *Le Mouvement social*, no. 92, July-September 1975.

A contributor under the name of Pierre Breton to *Le Parti ouvrier* (*The Workers' Party*), which was the daily organ of the allemanist party and a columnist for the "Journal de l'Etranger" ("Foreigner's Review") at *La Volonté* (*The Will*), which was a socialist daily founded by the young journalist Franklin-Bouillon in 1898, Herr was also one of the main founders of and an official editor for *L'Humanité* in 1904. For one year, he regularly provided articles on the second page about foreign policy.

Years later, when he became director of the Musée Pédagogique (Pedagogical Museum), he provided the *Journal de psychologie normale et pathologique* (Journal of Normal and Pathological Psychology) with a dozen very short book reviews between 1925 and 1926. Here, the corpus is limited to reviews for the *Revue critique d'histoire et de littérature* and the *Revue universitaire*. Partisan articles and comments on socialist meetings and international politics remain beyond the scope of direct interest; Herr himself chose to separate these two aspects of his life. The 200 or so pages that are available form a coherent, discreet corpus, one of the only ones that escapes Herrian fragmentation. As such, it constitutes in itself an object worthy of study. Moreover, as Andler points out, and as can be seen from the simultaneous reading of the two "texts" or sets of texts, the themes and style are close to what can be read in *Le Progrès et l'Affranchissement*. Moreover, Herr wrote these two kinds of texts during the same period, and a dialogue emerges quite naturally between them; *Progrès* and the reviews mutually illuminate one another and make it possible to further specify the contours of Herr's bibliographic and librarianship project.

What is it that these articles reveal? First, the examination of the book reviews makes it possible to confirm, "on results," so to speak, Herr's fabulous encyclopedic competence, and his astonishing reading ability. The reviewed works are written in French, English, German, Latin, Greek, Italian, and Russian about an extreme variety of themes as diverse as: history (both ancient or modern, Byzantine, and Western); philosophy (German and English; ancient and contemporary; analytical, Cartesian, and Rousseauian); music; archeology; epigraphy; geography; pedagogy; philology; literary history; religious history; economics; and sociology. The systematic analysis of these articles reveals the dimensions of the immense work Herr performed for his readers. Between January and May 1893, a period when both journals overlap, the number of reviews increases. 49 titles are listed for the month of January alone, 229 between January and May, and very few titles are found in both journals. From June 1893 to July 1894, 208 reviews by Herr were published in the *Revue universitaire* alone.

What is also striking is the difference in tone between the two journals, with the reviews not having the same objective from one to the next. In the *Revue critique d'histoire et de littérature*, articles are often more severe, sometimes downright cutting. The freedom of judgment in such a young man is also surprising. Herr was only 24 years old in 1888 when he started making contributions to the journal. Between 10 and 20 articles of his would appear in this journal per semester, extending over several pages and presenting meticulous analyses of books. In the *Revue universitaire*, the articles are shorter but more numerous. Herr himself defined the modalities of his critique in January 1893:

> There will be no mention here of textbooks, which have an obvious readership, books for a general audience, books that are quite bad, or works on very fine points of erudition, which interested parties are looking for and can find information about in specialized periodicals. Ideally, each issue of the *Revue* will mention the most important historical, philological, and philosophical works published the previous month. The book titles will be accompanied, when deemed useful, by a few lines intended to summarily state the content, and sometimes the shortcomings.[80]

Herr positioned himself as participating in a process of dissemination of knowledge and advice, but also of usage: to inform his readers of what was new and the progress of scholarly production and sort out "good readings," i.e. readings of high quality as well

---

80   *Revue universitaire*, January 1893, no. 6, p. 51

as what was "usable," or which texts lent themselves to enriching scholarly work.

In this statement, there are echoes of the aforementioned acquisition policy of Vidal de la Blache for the ENS library, and also the letter of 1905 in which Herr expresses his management principles for the library. Furthermore, the readers targeted by these reviews are neither academics nor the standard public for popular works, even of a high level, nor highly specialized scholars. They were thus Normaliens, students, and researchers. The bibliographer's activity appears to have been directly oriented towards the ENS library.

The Librarian Bibliographer

To confirm this perception of close solidarity between the two functions, we have carried out for the year 1893 a systematic comparison between the articles of the two journals, and the titles appearing in the register of acquisitions of the ENS library archives. 1893, as we have seen, was the most intense period of journalistic production for Herr.

This comparison has shown that there seems to have been a very real correlation between reviews and acquisitions. About one hundred books purchased in 1893 by the library had been the subject of a positive review by Herr in the same year. The approximation of the number of works purchased is due to the doubt that remains for certain cases: it appears that Herr was in the habit of using abbreviations to keep track of his entries. Works of epigraphy written in Latin, or of history written in German, often have titles that are quite similar to one another: "Inscript. Lat." for "Inscriptiones latinae" or "Gesch. For "Geschichte." The abbreviated notation adds to the confusion.

When reading the articles, we endeavored to attribute to each work a value corresponding to Herr's assessment: "excellent," "very good," "good," "no indication," or "to be avoided." If this ranking lacks an objective scale, it nonetheless makes it possible to establish that the vast majority of books purchased by the library following review received a very good assessment: this is the case for 53 of them (excellent or very good critique); 27 were considered "good" and, for 20 titles, only the publication is mentioned, without further details. None had received a negative assessment. It is likewise noteworthy that certain works in which Herr recognized scholarly interest, methodological merits, and clarity of expression, but for which he clearly communicated his interpretative or ideological disagreement, were purchased. This is the case, for example, of a German educational book purchased in May and entitled *Deutschlands Höheres Schulwesen im 19 Jahrhundert*, by a certain Rethwisch, which advocates for education that strictly adheres to Catholic principles. This substantiates the view that Herr was not attempting to make the ENS library a den of socialism.

Finally, it is almost certain that some entries do not appear on the register, but entered by way of donation from the journal, or authors, after reviews made by Herr. Indeed, from 1890 onwards, the register of acquisitions only indicates works that entered the collections as purchases, while early entries for the register (1888) indicate documents that were received as donations from authors or institutions. The different volumes of *L'Histoire générale* (*General History*), from the fourth century to the late nineteenth century, for which the publication (1892–1901) was overseen by Lavisse, and the corrections of which Herr was actively involved in,[81] received an excellent review when they were published. They appeared in the topographic catalog, but without any mention of the date of entry. These overlaps reinforce the hypothesis of a close connection between the two activities. However, the benefits of good reading materials were not confined to the shelves of the library.

Definition of a Critical Approach

Herr was too modest when he announced in January 1893 that "titles of books will be accompanied, when deemed useful, by a few lines intended to summarize the content." Even in the *Revue*

---

81   Proofs corrected by Herr can be consulted in carton LH1 dossier 8 in the Lucien Herr collection at the Centre d'Histoire de Sciences Po.

critique, articles were occasionally substantial and engaged veritable polemic discussions on equal terms with their authors. Reading the reviews makes it possible to bring out the major lines of a critical approach capable of discriminating the quality of books and that harbors very clear resonances with the fragments of *Progrès*. Writing articles seemed to be a concrete application of the project of critical thinking contained in *Progrès*. It is therefore particularly fruitful to conduct a parallel reading, so as to shed light on the thought of the librarian-bibliographer.

Developments in Critical Thinking

In these readings, it becomes quickly evident what Herr's criteria were for determining a work's quality. Almost all can be traced back to an evaluation of the author's conscientiousness in order to evaluate the reliability of the information provided or contentions asserted. First, any overwrought style was frequently noted and criticized. Herr was wary of literary affectation, which authors would employ to conceal shallow erudition or a lack of rigor. Severe irony often sanctioned the emptiness hidden behind the "joli" ("pretty"), to use the term used in *Progrès*: "The form is miserably flat, and the form is swollen and grandiloquent."[82] Or again: "A remarkable banality of mind was expressed in an unbearably ambitious and affected language."[83]

On the other hand, Herr's standards for bibliographic precision, reliability of sources, and their critical approach was very high. The methodological rigor of works was, from this point of view, very frequently subject to verification and analysis:

> What makes the value of Monsieur Baeumker's book
> sustainable and in some ways definitive is the prudent

---

82 Regarding Bruno Wille, *Philosophie der Befreiung durch des reine Mittel*, Berlin, 1894, in *Revue universitaire*, June 1894, no. 15, p. 186.

83 Regarding Charles Benoist, *L'Etat et l'Eglise*, in *Revue critique d'histoire et de littérature*, March 1893, p. 358.

> use it makes of texts and all texts. Monsieur B. has tak-
> en on the task of collecting, classifying, and critiquing
> with a precision that leaves nothing to be desired, infor-
> mation from all over that we possess regarding the the-
> ories about the ancient philosophers… There will be no
> need to ever do what he has done again.[84]

Herr recorded errors or information missing from bibliographies with extreme care. Thus, this surprising, but not uncommon, mention: "The bibliographic references are excellent and very accurate (except p.18, n.1, which does not exist)."[85]

It was indeed this inscription in a definite and verifiable bibliographic universe that was a guarantee that the work was serious and scholary. Finally, Herr scrupulously considered the text's method of exposition and its analytic organization. "A collection of this kind would be serviceable if it were easy to use, but Monsieur T. does not succeed in this regard. The physical layout of the work is a complication that makes it very difficult to use."[86] What is visible here is Herr's concern for the use that would be made of the book in question. Did the indexes, glossaries, and summaries, make the work practical and really usable? Whether they were designed with the intention for usage: this was the clue that books were not considered as finite entities, self-contained, but rather works open to their own surpassing, capable of lending themselves in good faith to their own critique or to their own enrichment. In other words, the books that Herr considered to be successful were those that took part in the ongoing march of Progress.

---

84 Regarding Clemens Baeumker, *Beiträge zur Geschichte der Philosophie des Mittelalters*, Bonn, 1891, in *Revue critique*, May 1892, p. 152.

85 Regarding George Adam Smith, *The historical geography of the Holy land*, London, 1893, in *Revue universitaire*, June 1894, p. 179.

86 Regarding Troost, *Zenonis Citiensis de rebus physicis doctrinae fundamentum*, 1892, in *Revue critique*, May 1892, p. 153.

Contextual Criticism

The commentary on the internal composition of the works was therefore an exercise of critical thought, teaching readers to exercise a scholarly perspective in their own readings so as to assess the author's reliability. This was the bibliographer's first lesson. The second, which required a formidable encyclopedic competence specific to Herr, was that of contextualization. One way to formulate the question that Herr answered in his critiques would be: How does this book position itself in the universal bibliography? In other words, what progress of knowledge does it advance?

We remember the importance of the "new idea" in the Herrian and Hegelian system of progress. It was the sign of the liberation of the mind, and of its movement towards a new way of thinking. Thus, in his review Herr was committed to identifying innovation. This was one of the main criteria that determined a book's quality:

> "The book of Monsieur P. Souriau is very rich in precise and new ideas, presented with an especially ingenious and clear method ... Some chapters are entirely new and perfect."[87]
>
> "... In particular, some chapters, like the one about Herder, the one about Fichte, the one about Frédéric Schlegel, are new and perfect."[88]

In order to identify innovation and progress as well as the significance of any steps forward, familiarity with the previous scholarship was necessary. In this regard, Herr's encyclopedic knowledge was indispensible. The librarian knew the contents of his books and the state of all disciplines. He thus often referred to a kind of general

---

87 Regarding Paul Souriau, *L'esthétique du mouvement*, Paris, Alcan, 1889, in *Revue critique*, September 1890, p. 517.

88 Regarding Richard Fester, *Rousseau und die deutsche Geschichtsphilosophie*, Stuttgart, 1890, in Revue critique, January 1892, p. 32.

state of a universal library's collection. For example: "Alfred Weber's book is the best history of philosophy that we possess in French."[89]

Once he had identified innovation, it was necessary to contextualize it so as to understand where it belonged in the collective edifice of progress. It is important to remember that the new idea was not progress itself; rather, it was the luminous center of progress as it advanced, incorporating and organizing the proper orientation of its own development. The bibliographer thus was to direct the march of progress. He revealed the ramifications of a way of thinking that was developing and expanding. For recent books, he would start by precisely identifying its field of research, then recall the competing interpretations that had preceded it; being careful to not judge authoritatively, he would offer advice about possible applications of the work, expressing his preferences for such applications but ultimately leaving readers to choose for themselves.

> Here is a new edition and a new commentary on the Coptic texts of the Bruce papyrus, which are of interest in the history of Gnosticism and the history of Neo-Platonism in Syria and Egypt. Unfortunately, Schmidt's interpretation differs from the recent work of Monsieur Amelineau regarding several essential points, and this will lead to confusion for those who are not Coptic specialists but who want to draw on these sources… It is conceivable that the abundant explanatory commentary by Monsieur Schmidt, which denotes a solid knowledge of Gnosticism, establishes a presumption in his favor. [90]

This approach dissects and classifies scholarly production so as to render it intelligible. As the author of reviews, Herr was not satisfied with developing a catalog to facilitate library acquisitions; the

---

89   Regarding Alfred Weber, *Histoire de la philosophie européenne*, Paris, 1892, in *Revue critique*, March 1892, p. 115.

90   Regarding Carl Schmidt, *Gnostische Schriften in koptischer Sprache*, Leipzig, 1892, in *Revue universitaire*, January 1893, p. 57.

reviews organized access to meaning by putting the works into dialogue with one another. The bibliographer also worked prospectively. His inventory and review work allowed him to signal what was missing and to instigate new works. He would call on the intellectual community for them:

> It is indisputable that at the moment, our knowledge of the philosophy of the Middle Ages can only progress through the association of many good and active individuals. The overall description is now complete. The execution of the details remains to be done nearly in its entirety. We have none of the tools that would be needed: critical works are lacking, attributions still need to be examined, the chronology of the works remains to be established, the editions themselves still need to be done or redone. The mass of works that are still unknown, or barely explored, lying dormant in libraries, is infinite.[91]

This applied bibliography was the realization of the project contained in *Progrès*. The bibliography asserted itself as the best weapon of critique; it was not solely a matter of the choice of books, but rather how the bibliography made it possible for the mind to not consider social constructions as natural but as elaborate human systems for the purposes of domination. The systematic analysis of the genesis of social phenomena made it possible to fight—first and foremost, to fight religion. "We have before us the complete genesis of a religion," Herr wrote in *Progrès*. "We know the precise literary and philosophical origins of it, the diplomatic and political motives."[92] In other words, it was possible to reconstitute the current state of religion in a bibliographic manner by looking at texts of the past. Performing this kind of genealogical work was to contextualize the texts, to unveil their true status, and, if necessary, be

---

91   Regarding Paul Correns, *Die dem Boethius faelschlich zugeschriebene*, in *Revue critique*, May 1892, p. 133.

92   Lucien Herr, op. cit., p. 20.

able to denounce them as scams. In this sense, it was in the library that the tools necessary for the liberation of humanity were located. A librarian assumed a role within the community of intellectuals. A fellow traveler along the road of human progress, the librarian identified and classified the scholarly output recorded in books so as to make it accessible and comprehensible. With the bibliography, the librarian made the mind conscious of itself, of its past, of its progress, of the deceptions it had overcome, and indicated new directions for further advancement.

The Counselor

The Editorial Secretary

From 1894 to 1904 Lucien Herr was a contributor to the *Revue de Paris*. Newly founded by the Calmann-Lévy publishing house, in 1893 the *Revue* called upon Ernest Lavisse to replace its scientific director. Lavisse, in need of an excellent editorial secretrary, turned to Herr based on his esteem for the lively reports in the *Revue universitaire* and the *Revue critique* that had caught his attention. The *Revue de Paris* then asserted itself as a competitor of the conservative *Revue des deux Mondes*, which had been under the direction of Ferdinand Brunetière since 1893. While the *Revue de Paris* was not revolutionary, it left room for new and liberal ideas. Nonetheless, members of the intellectual bourgeoisie were among the journal's readers.

Herr's position at the ENS library, which kept him in contact with young minds, made him especially qualified to identify young talents of importance. Informed of all the works that were coming to fruition, his role was to establish a link between Lavisse and the young researchers who represented the future of French scholarship. This position enabled Herr to situate himself upstream of scholarly production and to ensure that it was distributed in intellectual circles. Herr published the works of Ernest Renan as well as the historians Gabriel Monod and Alphonse Aulard. In addition, he was the first to introduce writings by Anatole Le Braz (1859–1925), an author and a Breton-speaking folklorist with whom Herr maintained a constant correspondence[93] while learning Breton and taking an interest in differences among the Celtic languages; Daniel Halévy (1872–1962), a historian, political scientist, and a member of the Académie des sciences morales et politiques (Academy of Moral Sciences and policies) who later became the director of collections at Grasset; Emile Mâle (1862–1954), a historian and Normalien who graduated in the same year as Herr; and Victor Bérard (1864–1931), also a Normalien, a specialist in Greek affairs and political columnist who gave the *Revue* articles on England's history and politics. Herr also brought in Romain Rolland (1866–1944), then a young talent, who provided the *Revue* with some of his first dramas.

However, the collaboration was not entirely free of turbulence. Although Herr had strong convictions and an authority granted by his status at the ENS, he didn't always have the final word. In 1903, he encouraged an author[94] to submit an article to him, ensuring the favor of the editorial board: "My dear friend, it is the right time to propose the article of which you speak, and it's been done; Lavisse is much looking forward to it. Tell me some time in advance when the article will be ready, and when would be a good time for it to be published."[95] Yet some time later, Herr had to find the words to communicate disappointing developments to the author:

> My dear friend, the bad news comes in droves. And it is just my luck to be the one who has to be the bearer of it, and who will be begrudged for having transmitted it… Lavisse is not happy with your article. He finds it vague and weak, empty, not clear, not well-considered … This will pain you, and it pains me to write to you of it.[96]

---

93   Lucien Herr Collection at the Centre d'Histoire de Sciences Po, LH1 Dossier 4.

94   The author could not be identified. The two letters in question are in Dossier 4 of carton LH3, which is supposed to contain the correspondence with Célestin Bouglé. But the tone and the information contained in these letters do not seem to fit with the usual content of the correspondence between Herr and Bouglé.

95   Letter of 1903, LH3 dossier 4.

96   Letter of 1903, LH3 dossier 4.

Disagreements, more political than academic in nature, had already begun by the time of the Dreyfus Affair, in which Herr was so involved. There was no trace of the event in the *Revue*. Neither Herr nor Lavisse could break this silence against the stance of the publisher, though Herr made efforts to make other voices heard. Before a general election, Jaurès was invited to speak alongside other major party leaders. Herr was met with refusal by the journal when he tried to publish excerpts from the *Histoire de la Révolution* (*History of the Revolution*) by Jaurès. This serious disagreement was the catalyst for his departure at the very end of January 1894. He barely had time to write a final letter to Celestin Bouglé:

> When the article is finished, send it here to the *Revue*, to Lavisse himself, or to Victor Bérard. I leave the *Revue* in eight days. I committed ten years of my life to something that could definitively reach an impasse. I am too old to continue to put so much work and energy into something that is too disproportionately distant from my ideas, my concerns, and my personal way of looking at useful action. I don't want to exhaust myself too long on tasks that are ultimately be in vain... And so I'm leaving, with a heavy heart, of course, but still happy that Lavisse has given me my freedom.[97]

The Reader-Advisor

Despite this unfortunate end, which, according to Andler, affected Herr greatly,[98] the participation in the *Revue* was beneficial insofar as it created or strengthened connections between Herr and scholars he would not have had the opportunity to meet at the ENS. The *Revue* had served as a springboard for certain collaborations, as was the case with Sébastien Charléty (1867–1945), who had his

---

97   Letter of January 23, 1904 to Célestin Bouglé, LH3 dossier 4.

98   Charles Andler, op. cit., p. 138.

agrégation in history and was not a Normalien. He specialized in Saint-Simonism and, after working as a professor at the faculty of literature in Lyon, became director of public instruction and fine arts in Tunis. The lively correspondence[99] between Herr and Charléty began in January 1902 and ended in 1926 when Herr died.

It all started in 1902, when Herr asked Charléty for the manuscript of his article that Lavisse had requested. The end of this short letter indicates that the two men had not yet met: Herr assured the historian that he "was still hoping and anticipating to meet [him] in person one day." It appears that the two men became friends a few years later. Herr wrote very long letters to Charléty and advised him about his work on the history of Saint-Simonism.[100] When Charlety met Herr, the admiration and gratitude he had for the breadth and precision of Herr's work was clear. "Your work inspires me with respect ... Nobody will ever read me like you have read me."[101]

In fact, Herr read the texts submitted to him twice ("I finished your first volume for the second time"[102]) before submitting his observations in the form of notes: "While reading, I noted all observations that your text inspired as they revealed themselves to me. I'm sending you the entire dossier directly. You will find it to be voluminous." Given the extreme precision with which Herr wrote his reviews, it is easy to imagine the quantity of observations returned to the author. It's also possible to gauge the speed at which he worked, as mentioned previously in regards to his reviews: scarcely a month later, on January 30, 1914, a second recommended letter was sent to Charlety. It read, "I finished reading your second

---

99   LH3 dossier 1.

100   Sébastien Charléty, *Histoire du saint-simonisme*, Hachette, 1931, based on the dissertation *Essai sur l'Histoire du saintsimonisme*, likewise published by Hachette in 1896.

101   Letter of December 26, 1913 to Lucien Herr, LH3 dossier 1.

102   Letter of December 23, 1913 to Sébastien Charléty, LH3 dossier 1.

volume. You will perhaps receive, at the same time as the manuscript, the comments I took note of while I was reading."[103]

What is interesting about this correspondence, which can be followed over several years, is that it shows a Herr who participated fully in the writing of books. If corrected volumes are not in the Lucien Herr archive, the letters summarize the directions that he wanted to see a work underway to take. These observations are not anecdotal, but rather call for entire parts that are still missing, identify gaps by putting several phenomena into perspective, and suggest elements of interpretation.

> In a general way, what struck me most (as a lacuna) is the brevity with which European affairs and history are indicated for our era. Not just the course of French history, which I believe requires a historical perspective—painted in broad strokes—of parallel movements, contemporary developments, exchanges of influence, developments in European opinion—but I believe that this would shed light on affairs external to France, and they would come to life and be easier to follow.

Though he was not the author of scholarly works himself, Herr helped to shape authors' thinking, making their ideas as incisive and new as possible. He would suggest ways to clear up real ramifications that had not yet been explored. The encouraging words he wrote to Charléty assume the same terms and the same themes that are in *Progrès* and in his works of critique: "I would have liked to have been able to take note of everything that was pleasing to me, that seemed strong, new, lucid, excellent… but this is not what you expect from me."[104] And, for the second volume:

"I read everything there is with great interest, especially the new ideas in the sections about economics and society, information

103   Letter of January 30, 1914 to Sébastien Charléty, LH3 dossier 1.

104   Letter of December 23, 1913 to Sébastien Charléty, LH3 dossier 1.

that had not been grouped together and clarified before, vividly foregrounding that which we thought we knew but only knew vaguely, and rendering intelligible that for which we only had a superficial and inexact representation."[105]

This passage exhibits the sense and the value that Herr gave to the "new" in the world of the intellect. We find the image of the new idea as a "luminous point of tension" that reorganizes knowledge around itself, thereby making it clearer. In sum, it is a matter of reclassifying information that we may already have but not really master because it is poorly arranged. The new idea is also a new method of classification and organization. Classification, and the logic of classification, renders things intelligible.

It would probably be fruitful to carry out a systematic study of the intellectual genealogy regarding the reading advice that Herr dispensed generously to his friends. It was not just a matter of methodological advice; the underlying question that Herr seemed to address was not "How to make this chapter clearer?" but "How to increase the power of thought that is at work here?" Andler emphasized many times that Herr was truly the co-author of many books published at the beginning of the century, yet the shyness and natural reserve that others have so frequently mentioned led him to refuse public recognition. Such a project would make it possible to shed light on the peculiarities of a scholarly co-authorship and would show us the librarian-philosopher's mind at work from within.

Lucien Herr, Multimedia Librarian?

In 1916, while remaining librarian of the ENS, Herr became director of the Musée Pédagogique (MP) and remained there until his death in 1926. Over the course of these ten years, he held both positions simultaneously and was thus in charge of two very different libraries. While the ENS had what was overall a classic research library, the MP was a polymorphous institution, a sort of laboratory where a new kind of library was being invented.

---

105   Letter of January 30, 1914 to Sébastien Charléty, LH3 dossier 1.

Context

Herr, Director of the Musée Pédagogique

In 1916, Jules Coulet, director of the MP, was appointed as rector of the academy of Grenoble. Paul Painlevé, the Minister of Education (1915–1917), asked Lavisse to appoint Herr as successor. Herr had already turned down and was yet to turn down many prestigious positions that would, by improving on his modest salary of 4,000 francs per year as librarian at the ENS, have enabled him to get out of the financial straits described by Andler.[106] These jobs included general inspector of libraries and archives, which was offered to him long before the war; the position of curator of the Bibliothèque Nationale; director of the Institut de Coopération Intellectuelle; and, finally, director of the Bibliothèque de l'Université, which he was long slated for and which the minister offered him in 1925. Herr's letter to Gustave Lanson, who had been the director of the ENS since 1919, is a testament to his determination:

> I saw the minister this morning, and it was just as I'd thought. He made me a solid offer. My decision was made, for serious reasons that he respected, though regretfully: the whole place was in ruins, he told me... in the end he gracefully conceded to my loyalty to the Ecole. I therefore remain faithful to you and to my task, and this gives me sincere joy.[107]

Herr, however, accepted the position as director of the MP. Andler points out that the geographical proximity of the MP, then located on rue Gay Lussac, made it possible for Herr to combine the two functions. Would Herr have also been motivated by the prospect of a well-paid position? The war had led to general poverty, and his second child had been born in 1915.

---

106   Charles Andler, op. cit., p. 281.

107   Archives Nationales, carton 61 AJ/157.

It is difficult to ascertain the motives that led Herr to accept this job in 1916, which forever doomed the possibility of scholarly output. In 1920, after four years of service, one thing is certain: Herr had a real vision for the museum, as evidenced by the strategic scope of the project. In the museum's administration, Herr occupied a place at the center of the debates that were causing great upheaval in the world of education and also, in a more limited manner that was still just as dramatic, the world of libraries.

Birth and Development of the Musée Pédagogique

There had been discussion of setting up a scholastic or educational museum in France since the mid-nineteenth century. The programs that ensued were vast but somewhat disorganized. All aimed to create a place dedicated to the history of education in France, with a museum component to bring together reference books on the subject, pedagogical articles (chalkboards, tools, teaching materials), manuals, and surveys, as well as a kind of institute dedicated to the research and comparison of teaching methods in different countries, with the aim of improving the French system. The decisive impetus was provided by Jules Simon, who was the Minister of Public Instruction in 1871. The initial collection included books, chalkboards, and tools for use by schools, including books and scholastic implements employed in foreign countries. Rectors were requested to have lists made of books, local monographs, regulations, and statistics relating to primary schools for the public libraries under their jurisdiction. But everything was suddenly abandoned with the departure of the minister in May 1873, which brought the enterprise to a halt.

Five years later, Ferdinand Buisson, who was then the head of the statistics and primary education department at the Ministère de l'Instruction, studied the functioning of pedagogical museums abroad, and proposed the creation in France of an analogous museum. The MP was created by decree, under Ferry as minister, on May 13, 1879. The essential provision of the decree states that:

"A pedagogical museum and a central library of primary education is created at the Ministère de l'Instruction Publique. This museum includes various collections of scholastic materials, historical and statistical documents, and instructional books from France and abroad."[108] Associated with the pedagogical museum was the Bibliothèque centrale de l'enseignement primaire (Central Library of Primary Education), which was in charge of collecting educational statistics.

When it first started out, the museum therefore had four sections: scholastic tools; teaching materials; central library (books for teachers, books for pupils, school libraries, popular libraries); and documents relating to the history of education. Throughout its history, the MP has undergone many changes. With an initial period of growth up to the early 1930s, its services multiplied. The MP diversified its activities to address the multiple dimensions of education and to adapt to all the needs of an educational community that was immersed in deep self-reflection.

• 1882: creation of the "circulating library," comparable to a remote lending service.

• 1885: publication of works or documents relating to public education, with the title *Mémoires et documents scolaires*. Due to lack of funds, the series of publications stopped in 1892.

• 1886: Ferdinand Buisson also wanted the MP to be the center of oral instruction so as to inform the French public about the state of institutions in different European countries. Finally, preparatory sessions were instituted for the educational aptitude certification exam (created in 1886), and the examination for teachers at the *écoles normales*, which are French institutions where instructors and scholars of all kinds prepare for their profession, and *écoles primaires supérieures*, which served to supplement students' regular coursework at primary schools. In Herr's time, the proximity to the ENS made it possible to organize preparatory conferences for the *aggrégation* at the museum.

• 1891: the MP became a place of exhibits, both permanent and temporary. The first permanent exhibition was requested by the

---

108   Text reproduced in *Revue pédagogique*, first semester of 1879.

minister and displayed student notebooks from all regions of France for a single school year. This exhibit, a kind of glimpse into the life at the nation's schools, presented visitors with children's and teachers' programs and work methods.

- 1896: creation of the Service des Vues et des Projections lumineuses (Illuminated Slides and Projections Service).

- 1903: by the decree of March 31, 1903, the Musée Pédagogique and the Bibliothèque Centrale de l'Enseignement Primaire (Central Library for Primary Education) combined with the Office de l'Information et d'Études (Office of Information and Study), created in 1901. The museum then took the name of "Musée pédagogique, bibliothèque, office et musée de l'enseignement public" (Pedagogical Museum, Library, Office, and Museum for Instruction of the Public). The same decree expanded the museum's responsibilities, which now focused on all levels of public education (primary, secondary, higher education), and ceased to be exclusively for primary education.

- 1904: the Office acquired the "assistants" service, which organized the exchange of assistants, or tutors, between educational institutions in France and abroad. The exchanges were primarily with England, Austria, Scotland, and Italy; after the war, relations were slowly renewed with Germany, and started with the United States.

- 1919: Service of Vues Fixes (Stationary views) started.

- 1920: School Cinematograph Service started.

Starting in the 1930s, acquisition credits decreased. The museum moved to the rue d'Ulm. Reforms led to the establishment in 1932 of the Centre national de documentation pédagogique (National Center of Pedagogical Documentation), under the influence of which educational research progressed in the years following the Second World War.

After the annexation of the Centre international d'Etudes pédagogiques et du Centre national d'enseignement par correspondance (International Center for Pedagogical Studies and the National Center for Education through Correspondence), the institution assumed the name of Institut Pédagogique National (National Pedagogical Institute), or IPN, in 1956. The IPN brought together historical collections and provided informational and documentation services for teachers. In 1970, the IPN was divided into two parts: the Institut National de la Recherche et de la Documentation Pédagogique (National Institute of Research and Pedagogical Documentation), and the Office Français des Techniques Modernes d'Education (French Office of Modern Techniques of Education). In 1976, the Institut National de Recherche Pédagogique (National Institute of Pedagogical Research), or INRP, was established and reaped a dual legacy as a site for hosting and developing research and a resource center for documents regarding education.

The split of 1980 led to the situation we know today. Documents of a museographic character, bringing together books, objects, and images, were attributed to the Musée de l'Histoire de l'Education (Museum of the History of Education) in Rouen. Books and periodicals are at the INRP Library, located in Lyon since 2005. Finally, the more archival documents were transferred to the national archives.

The problem of sources

Paradoxically, the MP is a particularly amnesic institution. Unfortunately, this is the case especially for the period (1916–1926) that concerns us.[109] The brief introductory text that opens the archive's inventory in the general summary of resources at the National Archives makes mention of the very incomplete state of these archives. With the situation characterized by both abundance of activity and lack of sources, it is difficult to determine the influence of Herr's management at the museum. However, it is possible to make attempts, based on the restricted sources and contexts of the time, to retrace the shape

---

109   On this topic, see Nelly Kuntzmann, *Des images pour le dire, des mots pour le voir. Prémisses de la culture audiovisuelle,* éducation *et bibliothèque, 1895–1940,* Mémoire DCB, ENSSIB, 1995, p. 84.

that his leadership gave to this multiform institution, along with the promise this great behemoth seemed to hold for him.

As for primary sources, there are six internal reports made to the institution. The documents written by Herr are a report for 1920; a note dated March 8th of the same year concerning the glass slides; a report for 1924 as well as a "Note on the slides and films service" dated October 31, 1924; and a report for 1925. We also have a report for 1926–1927, signed by Lebrun, who was Herr's successor. This last report offers an interesting counterpoint to the previous documents and makes it possible to more specifically identify Herr's position.[110] A letter of 1920 addressed to Andler also provides valuable information. Herr's successor was in favor of refocusing the museum around "classic" activities (museum and library), and in opposition Herr defended a multifaceted conception of the institution with "the desirable extension of the different services."[111] What he wanted was to keep the different services together; they corresponded to the different functions of an ideal library: reference books for a study library (central library); conservation (legal deposit); expanded distribution through remote loan (circulating library); documentation and information (Office); promotion of new media (services of slides and cinematography); and affirmation of the museum as the leader of a regionalization a new library model.

An Instrument of Social Progress

The letter in which Herr reveals to Andler his program for the museum dates from October 27, 1920.[112] The allusion is short; is it a real project, or just a dream of an ideal institution? It's hard to say. In any case, the details are precise enough to provide a framework for analysis, or at least elements for interpretation, of his activities as director:

---

110 All of these documents are in the Musée Pédagogique collection at the Archives nationales, in carton 71 AJ 2.

111 Report of May 7, 1920 addressed to the Monsieur le Directeur de l'Enseignement primaire (director of primary instruction).

112 Antoinette Blum, op. cit., lettre 76, p. 183.

> You know just as well as I do that the serious problem
> with the Collège de France is the fatal rupture with
> young people. You will invent a public, but it will be
> comprised of amateurs, some specialists, rubberneck-
> ers, and strangers. Whether it will be a true field of ac-
> tion, nobody can tell. And these are matters where it's
> necessary that useful action be immanent, immediate.
> It would be best if a pedagogical institute with the free-
> dom for movement, flexible and independent enough to
> group individuals of all social classes and with all types
> of education, were annexed to the Sorbonne as a research
> laboratory for the necessary reforms and renovations.
> This would be the germ around which the organization
> of tomorrow would develop … This would all be perfect-
> ly in place at the Musée Pédagogique.

Herr suggests here that he wants a reform that would break down
the barriers between the different orders of education, which posed
obstacles to any form of real democratization. The museum would
be a place of study, documentation, and dissemination of information, thereby serving to guide the kinds of reflections that would in-
sert themselves into the great debate of the 1920s about the "Ecole
unique" and, more broadly, the vast movement for the reorganiza-
tion of education that began with the Third Republic.

In fact, during the nineteenth century the juxtaposition
of schools for notables and schools for the people translated to a
social structure with clear boundaries. The Third Republic trig-
gered a questioning of the entrenched distinction made between
the two orders of education, the *primaire* (primary) for the people,
and the *secondaire* (secondary) for the elites. These two systems did
not form successive degrees of the same education; rather, each order was a complete and self-contained system. Since the Guizot law
of 1833, the "communale," as primary school was called, had its
EPS (Ecole primaire supérieure). This intermediate course of study,
which lasted three years, was created for the emerging middle class.
It served as preparation for intermediate professional positions such
as schoolmasters or skilled workers. The EPS was entirely separate
from the paid secondary education reserved for elites, who did not

do their *petites classes* in primary school but in elementary classes, sometimes called the "petit lycée," at the *lycée* (high school).[113] The border between both orders was impermeable, and this problem of structure doubled as a pedagogical quarrel between the *Anciens* and the *Modernes*. The teaching of Latin was selective and prohibited all movement from one order to the next; compulsory in the *secondaire*, it was not taught in the *primaires*, nor in the EPS.[114]

This operation was as undemocratic as it was irrational, since it entrusted similar tasks to different organizations and promoted the selection of the Republic's elites on the basis of money. The debate spread during the period between the World Wars and related simultaneously to the unification of schooling by substituting degrees for orders, and to general free access to secondary instruction. The *Ecole unique* was promoted by the socialist party and the radical party. Herr was a staunch partisan of the most radical position that believed that all compulsory education, meaning education up to the age of 13, should be *unique* (mixed) and free. The opposition of several irreconcilable conceptions delayed the actualization of this project. In 1928, almost 50 years after the Ferry laws were passed to decree primary school as free and compulsory, the decision was finally passed to make secondary school free of charge.

It is necessary to consider Herr's activities as director of the MP within this context. We will see that his letter of 1920 is contemporary with two other documents in which he set out different projects for museum services. There was a convergence of his views on education and his professional endeavors, which participated in the same overall project of renewal by way of this very unique institution as well as the libraries. Later documents (1924–1926) seem less optimistic, though they do not dismiss Herr's visions as failures.

---

113   Antoine Prost, *Histoire de l'enseignement en France 1800–1967*, Colin, Paris, 1970, p. 405.

114   Pierre Merle, *La démocratisation de l'enseignement*, La Découverte, Paris, 2009, p. 16–26.

As soon as it was created, the library had a considerable collection thanks to the acquisition of the Rapet collection. Honorary Inspecteur Général of Primary Education Jean-Jacques Rapet (1805–1882), who had devoted fifty years of his life to gathering a collection of documents about public education and pedagogical books, had decided to get rid of his library. Ferry had had a law voted through on June 5, 1880 to authorize the MP's acquisition of the Rapet library. It consisted of approximately 5,500 titles and formed a near-exhaustive collection of publications relating to education, especially primary school, that had been published in France, Germany, Italy, England, and the United States. It also included a unique collection of foreign journals.

In addition to this inherited collection, following the foundational decree of May 13, 1879, the library also included historical works on education, statistics, and textbooks. A policy for purchasing textbooks and pedagogical books was set up almost immediately. The successive ministers of public education encouraged scholastic publishers to systematically provide the MP with the works they published and a system for exchanging books was established with the MP's foreign counterparts. The collection grew steadily.

The reports available in the MP's archives provide information about the central library's activities in 1920, 1924, and 1925. The 1920 report states that reading on-site was "unconditionally, entirely public," unlike the loan services or exam preparations, both of which were reserved for members of public education. Though it is not absolutely certain that free access to on-site resources is attributable to Herr, it is still possible to observe that the first statutes of the museum's library reserved this consultation only to members who were also in a position to borrow materials. The expansion of access corresponded to the way in which Herr managed the library at the ENS, leaving readers to move freely among the stacks.

The figures in these reports allow us to sketch a quick portrait of the library, but the incomplete state of the archives prevents us from actually charting its progress. For example, we have the approximate number of volumes (nearly 100,000) maintained by the library for 1920; then, for the 1924 financial year, the report indicates "an increase of 1650 works." The 1925 report does not provide information regarding the number of acquisitions made.

From one year to the next, the number of members remains roughly the same (1091 in 1924, 1046 in 1925), as does the number of loans made on-site (from 7,080 to 7,927) or from home (12,030 to 12,274). A very slight decrease is observable for loans made from home and for the number of members, with a more significant increase signaling the success of on-site consultation.

Herr's efforts to interpret the use of the collections for the 1924 financial year is more interesting. It denotes real attention to usages and readers. In comparing the loan figures for the different months of the year, he noted irregularities for home loans: they peaked during the months preceding the exams (March, April, May) and fell back down during the school holidays. The loans for on-site consultation were more regular and less affected by exam schedules. Several uses therefore coexisted for the library, which "respond[ed] perfectly to its purpose" of preparation for on-site consultation along with university competitions and exams.

In terms of the MP library, Herr's great achievement was, above all, the legal deposit of textbooks. He advocated for designating the MP as the legal depository of primary school textbooks, and several reports have been written to this effect.[115] The law of November 19, 1925 established the Central Library of Public Education (Bibliothèque Centrale de l'Instruction Publique) as the repository of the legal deposit of primary education textbooks. However, it was only through a simple verbal agreement with the Sainte-Geneviève library that Herr, a few days before his death (June 28, 1926), ensured that secondary school textbooks, legally assigned to the Sainte-Geneviève library, would be donated to the Central Library

---

115   "Les manuels scolaires à l'INRP," Resource dossiers on this history of education, http://www.inrp.fr/vst/Dossiers/Histoire/manuels.htm. The existence of these reports is certain, but they could not be located.

of Primary Education (Bibliothèque Centrale de l'Instruction Primaire): pursuant to the agreement, university textbooks were—and still are today—attributed to the Sainte-Geneviève library.

The Circulating Library

Established in 1882 as an annex to the Central Library, this service offered by the MP would send books on loan for free via parcel post all throughout France and Algeria for a period of two months, with a limit of three books at a time. This service was for anyone who could prove they were preparing for a pedagogical exam by presenting a certificate from the inspector of the academy or the primary inspector (inspecteur primaire). A loan could be renewed indefinitely. There were three divisions: letters, science, and education. The first collection included 200 books and by 1920 had reached 700. Herr described its formation with these words in 1920: "general works and textbooks providing an understanding of the current state of knowledge in its principal areas—popular works—and books of a more specific educational and pedagogical character designed to enable preparation for primary instruction." These were therefore works to assist in the preparation for competitive exams, but also works for those involved in higher education "who have the desire to learn and to improve themselves." At the central library, works were selected from among those most likely to fulfill this dual mission. In 1921, a catalog specific to the circulating library was created.

Herr seemed particularly attached to this service, which represented the realization of a social ideal: to make knowledge accessible to all. The diffusionist ideal borne by this library filled him with enthusiasm. The 1920 report mentions the major project of the "complete overhaul and expansion" of this "special work," for which the MP had received financial assistance. For Herr, the circulating library was the representative of a new model, the "first version of the model working library, lively, flexible, constantly updated, new, and efficient, which may, after a few years of trials and improvements, become the standard library and serve as an example to regional circulating libraries, the libraries of the *Ecoles normales*, and, to a certain extent, intercommunal libraries."[116] For there were circulating libraries already burgeoning in certain French *départements*, linked in particular to school libraries.[117] Herr envisioned a pioneering role for his own library that would serve as the head of a network and as a primary model. There was some overlap in terms of the most contemporary concerns of a working library and a public library.

The reports of 1924 and 1925 show that the financial assistance provided for the development of the library did not entirely pay off. "Due to insufficient funds," the number of copies available for each title of the circulating library remained fewer than needed, and the requirement to update the collection could not be fulfilled. The same authors remained in demand, and the long duration of the loan period made it difficult to rotate borrowed books. However, the figures speak for themselves in attesting to the vitality and success of the circulating library. We do not know the number of copies for these two years, but keeping in mind the 700 works of 1920, the figures are impressive: 4,785 for 1924 and 5,775 for 1925 for loans; about 400 loans per month, with highs of over 700 for the months preceding exams. The large number of unfulfilled requests indicates that things had not yet caught on outside of Paris and that the library of the MP remained the main provider of documents for those preparing for exams.

The Office of Documentation

The Golden Age of Documentation

In 1903, the MP merged with the Office d'informations et d'études (Office of Information and Research), which had been created in 1901. The task of the latter was to gather, classify, and list official documents and other documents to communicate the legislation

---

116   Report of 1920.

117   Jean Hebrard, "Les bibliothèques scolaires: l'impossible pari des bibliothèques circulantes," in Dominique Varry (dir.): *Histoire des bibliothèques françaises*, Vol 3, *Les bibliothèques de la Révolution et du 19ème siècle*, Paris, Cercle de la la Librairie, 2009, p. 741–45.

and administration of French public education abroad, and to collect this information from abroad to inform the Ministère public (public ministry). In addition, this office was responsible for conducting surveys regarding matters up for discussion and to publish the results. The world of education had in fact been undergoing profound renewal since the defeat of the 1848 Revolution, and then since the defeat of 1870. The university reform of the late nineteenth century deeply upset the traditional landscape. It offered expanded resources to establishments, opened new sections, created *agrégation* scholarships, and transformed *facultés* into universities by giving them a civic character, which promoted their capacity for innovation. This led to an increase in the workforce, a diversification of the public (women and foreigners in particular), and broader recruitment for higher education.[118] Similarly, the Ferry laws related to the *primaire* filled classrooms, creating new practices and new courses of study. An organization responsible for collecting information to understand, measure, and evaluate the scope of the various reforms and to prepare new ones thus seemed essential. In any case, this fusion made the MP a forerunner in the golden age of documentation.

An initial phase of innovation between 1880 and 1919[119] witnessed the growth and increasing prominence of documentary activities. Developments in both theory and practice led to this new relationship to information. First of all, there was a realization in professional circles (emerging industries, enterprises) and institutions (administrations, universities) of the need for specialized information. Organizations of various kinds to meet this need—specialized libraries, agencies, documentation centers–were multiplying. The synthesis between the MP's library and the Office created a modern facility with services that allowed several positions to complement one another.

---

118   Christophe Charle, Jacques Verger, *Histoire des universités*, PUF, Paris, 2007, p. 87–98.

119   Bruno Delmas, "Une fonction nouvelle: genèse et développement des centres de documentation," in Martine Poulain (dir.), *Histoire des bibliothèques françaises*, Vol 4: *Les Bibliothèques au 20ème siècle, 1914–1990*, p. 239–61.

The tremendous growth of scientific and technical information and the acceleration of production led to criticisms from scholars who believed that libraries were becoming storehouses where books piled up without the necessary access to content.[120] The problem was particularly acute for scientific periodicals: it was too slow to produce books to keep up with disciplines that were advancing quickly. Thus, it was up to periodicals to chart their progress: the challenge for libraries was to pare down and to update information immediately so as to make the new vehicle for scholarly research— now the journal article rather than the monograph—accessible.

However, the new representation of information truly emerged between 1895 and 1914, under the impetus of great figures such as Paul Otlet (1868–1944). 1895 was the year of the founding of the Institut International de bibliographie (International Blibliography Institute), created in Brussels by Otlet together with Henri Lafontaine (1854–1943). Overseeing theoretical and technical research related to international bibliographic cooperation, the aim of this institute was the organization of the Répertoire Bibliographique Universel, or RBU (Universal Bibliographic Repertory). Otlet provided an extensive definition of the term "information":

> What we mean by the general term 'information' is data of any kind, facts, ideas, and new theories, which, apprehended by the human intellect, constitute notions, clarifications, and guidelines for conduct and action; on the other hand, by documentation we refer to all the means specific to the transmission, communication, and dissemination (books, periodicals, newspapers, circulars, catalogs, texts and images, documents of all kinds) of information.[121]

---

120 Sylvie Fayet-Scribe, *Histoire de la documentation en France, Culture, science et technologie de l'information 1895–1937*, CNRS, Paris, 2000, p. 41.

121 "L'information et la documentation au service de l'industrie," *Bulletin de la Société d'encouragement pour l'industrie nationale*, May-June 1917, p. 517–47, cited by Sylvie Fayet- Scribe, op. cit., p. 75.

This was the realization that information constituted the whole of global intellectual production and was dispersed across a variety of media. Documentation was therefore the action of organizing information in the appropriate way so as to facilitate its communication.

Herr as Documentalist

The first function of the Office's service within the Museum was therefore to keep up to date on what was transpiring in scholastic matters outside of France (legislation, administration, programs, reforms) in order to provide clarification to French and foreign administrations as well as to the public. Herr therefore attempted to organize at the Office an exchange of documents between France and foreign countries, thus favoring cooperation over the purchase of documents; in any case, the latter was infeasible due to the institution's meager funds. In his first note of March 1920, remitted to the Chamber of Deputies Commission of Foreign Affairs, Herr points to the insufficiency of documentary resources and calls for a regular supply of documentation:

> It is essential that all documents touching directly or indirectly on teaching (statistics, directories, journals, newspapers, parliamentary reports, and administrative reports) be provided regularly, with enough copies to purposefully solicit an exchange service. We are in this respect entirely impoverished. When the British minister asks us for an official document, we are unable to satisfy his request.

In his letter to Andler, Herr expressed his wishes for this service to provide crucial support of and direction for research. The documentation feature was of paramount importance since it accelerated the dissemination of new ideas. "More than ever," he emphasized, "it will be indispensible to follow, day by day, the immense movements that are leading the whole world down the path of social renewal in public education."

But how to organize this information, to make it accessible? This was the role of the survey service, responsible for counting the specialized periodicals that the MP subscribed to, both from France and abroad, along with books and official documents. The service developed documentary products intended to provide well-designed access to this information: records were updated daily and reports about educational matters were established.

Herr was aware of the high level of technical know-how required by this "incessant and daily task of reading, counting, referencing, classifying, and critiquing in addition to quick, reliable writing and publishing as needed." At the end of his 1924 report, he emphasized the professionalism of his "excellent" staff members, though he expressed a desire to have more of them. Indeed, the Office was overseen only by an archivist and an assistant archivist. The MP needed "educated, long-term personnel," with a stability that would be encouraged through an acknowledged status and superior treatment:

> At the present time, it is isn't practical to aim to have graduates as assistant archivists or assistant librarians, since the maximum salary they could make is 4,500 francs less than what they would make teaching at a Collège. If we do not prescribe the measures that are of blinding urgency, it can be expected that in the near future the Musée will be abandoned by its officials and that hiring the suitable recruits will be forever an impossibility.

He was to prevail in this matter, since the *loi de finances* (finance act) of July 13, 1925 merged the MP and the central administration personnel.

The Slides and Films Service

The slides and films service started in 1920: from its inception, the educational cinematograph service was entrusted to the Service des Vues fixes et des Projections lumineuses (Stationary Views and Projections Department), which had existed at the museum since 1896. This service brought together the museum's collections of audiovisual works. The originality and modernity of this service was of course due to the fact that it oversaw media that were not very well developed in France, and especially to the importance given to the distribution of plates and reels. The collections were constituted and maintained for lending purposes. This feature responded perfectly to the missions of the museum, created in order to promote new educational initiatives and to be a "living organ of primary education, an instrument of action and progress."[122] The dynamic character of the institution contributed significantly to the development of the understanding and use of these new forms of media in the complex network of pedagogical materials (popular education and schools throughout the territory).

The Glass Slides Service

The creation of this service was a ministerial initiative that aimed to encourage the development of popular education. It was particularly successful in the final decades of the nineteenth century: the combined action of the state and multiple private initiatives (popular education societies, elected representatives, teachers, philanthropists) offered adolescents and adults additional education. In 1894, the government decided to give new impetus to these courses. A report was made[123] that described an overview of the situation of this instruction in France and recommended that a commission be formed to examine ways for providing access to light projection devices and collections of photographs that could be useful for public lectures. Light projections indeed ensured great success for lectures because of their novelty. In a circular of November 11, 1896, the minister urged local officials to redouble their efforts to stimulate the development of adult courses, and invited them to make use of the MP, which he had just entrusted with the loan service and the

---

122   Jules Steeg, "Le Musée pédagogique," *Revue pédagogique*, second semester 1896, p. 42.

123   Edouard Petit, "Cours d'adolescents et d'adultes. Les oeuvres complémentaires de l'école, l'éducation populaire en 1895–1896, rapport adressé au ministre de l'Instruction publique," *Revue pédagogique*, Semester 3 1896, p. 104 et seq.

dissemination of glass slides throughout the entire territory.[124] The "clients" for the slides, as Herr called them in his reports, quickly diversified: teachers promptly called on the MP for their use in the classroom; and during the war, the MP also supplied the French Army, which organized educational sessions in health centers, hospitals, soldier's homes, and military training centers.

The first collection was made up of donations from three societies particularly active in the field of popular lectures: the Ligue de l'Enseignement (League of Education), the Société havraise d'enseignement par l'aspect (Le Havre Society of Visual Education), and the Société nationale d'enseignement (National Society for Popular Education). Herr indicated in his 1924 report that a collection of 11,000 slides, a donation from the ministry, was added to this first collection. The development of the collection is not really detailed in the reports. The minimum guideline was for it to obey an encyclopedic representation of knowledge. But the collection also benefitted from opportunities that arose or that were created. The 1924 report mentions two important collections that were gained following the war and acquired by the MP. Were they free of charge, or expensive? The report does not say. In any case, a "good number of photographs prepared by the photographic section of the army and by the propaganda service" as well as a "considerable reserve of very beautiful shots liquidated by US services" (YMCA) were acquired.

The MP organized the documentary processing of these collections and a special commission on slides was created in 1896. With the support of the staff overseeing the slides services (10 people in 1924, making it the museum's largest department), which listed, prepared, and processed shipments, the commission served to select topics and to designate the appropriate authors to write the *notices*. Methodical work was performed on the slides when they entered the collections. Arranged by 20 or 30 in boxes specially

---

124 Armelle Sentilhes, "L'audiovisuel au service de l'enseignement: Projections lumineuses et cinéma scolaire, 1880–1940," *La Gazette des Archives*, 2nd Quarter 1996, no.173, p. 165–83.

designed for transport, they would comprise different series, available most frequently in ten copies (for 1924 at least). They were divided by subject, or by collection, of which there were 1600. In 1924, the museum recorded some 200,000 photographs, versus 32,600 in 1897. The catalog of slides was divided into sections organized for the encyclopedic representation of knowledge:

- Series A: History, Fine Arts, and Literature
    (240 subjects representing 3,315 boxes);
- Series B: Geography, Travel
    (245 subjects representing 2,395 boxes);
- Series C: Science (358 subjects representing 3,770 boxes);
- Series D: Social Sciences;
- Series E: Expositions.[125]

In Science, we find, for example, series on: Pasteur; Microbes; Ceramics; Milk. In Social Sciences: Insurance and Mutuals; Holiday Camp; Public Assistance in Paris under the Ancién Regime. In History, Fine Arts, Literature: A Visit to the National Archives; General Assemblies and the Constituent Assembly; Cluny Museum.

The catalog was sent free of charge to members of the teaching profession or to qualified individuals who had requested it. Thanks to an agreement with the Ministère des Postes (Ministry of the Postal Service), slides were also shipped free of charge.

The *notices* were booklets of about twenty pages which included a general presentation of the subject followed by commentary for each of the individual slides. They were included in the boxes for the lecturer or the instructor who was borrowing them, and they were designed in response to the numerous complaints about insufficient information provided about the slides. These *notices* constituted a valuable teaching tool for the development of a lesson. Kuntzmann's research has made it possible to identify the authors of the *notices*: 236 contributors wrote the 653 *notices* published

---

125   Report of 1925.

between 1898 and 1925. These were most often specialists in the various subjects. While educators and librarians did write them on occasion, it was with far less frequency. Primarily, the authors consisted of instructors of all levels, from schoolteachers to professors; engineers; servicemen, especially officers who were also skilled in geography; and doctors for matters related to anatomy, hygiene, and health.[126] However, the collections were also enriched according to the opportunities that arose or that were created.

Kuntzmann showed that a period of intense activity marked the rhythm of the production of views between 1898 and 1909, followed by a sharp decline in the production of *notices*.[127] Initially attributable to the war, the slowdown in activity did not cease, however, in 1918. And even for the 1921–1922 period, no new glass slides were made. Kuntzmann does not provide an explanation for this phenomenon in this document, nor does Herr mention it in his reports. However, when reading these reports, it's possible to draw the conclusion that "the increase in the price, the costliness of glass and impressions" that Herr deplores as it "sets us against narrow limitations and sadly hinders our action" may be to blame. Similarly, 1920 was the year that the cinematograph of the Ecole was created at the MP, and it's easy to imagine that this new activity detracted in part from the service's resources.

At any rate, the success of the glass slides service was very considerable for a period of twenty years. The increase in loans was constant from year to year until the start of the war: 8,859 loans for the 1896–1897; 22,630 only two years later (1898–1899); 31,915 in 1903–1904; 36,312 for 1913–1914. The activity of the service naturally abated during the war, as Herr indicates in his reports. Starting in the 1920s, Herr gladly welcomed the resumption of activity for the service. However, a graph published by the Service des Vues in 1929[128] detailing the number of slides and films made by

---

126 Nelly Kuntzmann, op. cit., p. 44.

127 Nelly Kuntzmann, op. cit, p. 48.

128 This graphic is reproduced in the article by Armelle Sentilhes, op. cit.

the museum between 1896 and 1928 shows a slow recovery starting in 1918. The number of loans increased until 1926, but without ever reaching the level it was at prior to the war. Herr himself indirectly furnishes the explanation: for lack of sufficient funds, the collection of slides could not be "enriched and renewed" as he required. "There needs to be new series, and the old series and the obsolete or out-of-date series need to be redone," so that this first-rate instrument would "not quickly lose its effectiveness and value."[129] The service, however, maintained its dynamic nature. The graph shows a new factor from 1920: the appearance of the film collection at the museum. The number of loans for this new medium increased steadily until 1928, to the point of meeting and then exceeding the shipments of the slides. During the financial year of 1927–1928, nearly 44,000 films were loaned out, versus only 32,000 slides. The films thus asserted themselves as a true competitor to the glass slides.

The Cinematograph of the Ecole

The idea of using film for educational purposes originated prior to World War I. In the 1910s, some pioneers were starting to advocate for the development of organizations to preserve and distribute educational films. In 1912, Leon Riotor (1865–1946), Vice-President of the Conseil municipal de Paris (Paris City Council) and the Conseil général de la Seine (General Council of the Seine), expressed his desire for the creation of a cinematheque that would serve the schools of Paris.[130] It was in 1915 that the initiative became a governmental one. Convinced perhaps by the successful use of glass slides in classes, and anticipating especially the immense efforts that public schooling would need to make once the war ended, the ministry instituted an extra-parliamentary committee called

---

129   Report of May 7, 1920.

130   Cited by Christophe Gauthier, *A l'école de la mémoire. La constitution d'un réseau de cinémathèques en milieu scolaire 1899- 1928*, Mémoire DCB, ENSSIB, 1997, p. 33.

the Cinématographe de l'Ecole (Educational Cinematograph) on March 23, 1916 as the war was still raging. This committee would be responsible for finding the best ways to generalize the use of cinematographs in the different branches of education. In his report to the President of the Republic, the minister set out clearly the reasons which justified this commission and indicated what role it should play. "After the War, the Ecole nationale (National School) will have to do more important work than in the past, and it will be responsible for hastening and increasing the nation's intellectual and moral development of the country."[131]

The Bessou report announcing the results of the commission's work was submitted in 1920. It affirmed the need to generalize educational assistance with the cinematograph in disciplines that had to encompass most of the fields of knowledge: biology, physics, history, geography, etc. He also recommended that exceptional credits be granted to support the acquisition of projection devices in the schools of France.

It is, it seems, at Herr's initiative that the ministry decided to create the educational cinematograph service at the museum. This is indicated in the 1926–1927 report of his successor; his own subsequent reports suggest that he had written notes to this effect for the minister, using the great skill already possessed by the slides service in the preservation of images as an argument. The new service was in fact growing very quickly. It was responsible for setting up a collection of films and copies for loan. The 1929 graph shows a rapid increase in loans of films: 3,521 for the year of its commissioning, nearly 20,000 two years later, and 44,000 for 1927–1928. These numbers attest to its vitality and, as previously mentioned, its direct competition with the slides service. The museum's success becomes even more obvious when we consider the number of loans in light of the number of films owned. The notice on the slides service for 1924 indicates 2,182 films owned that year. Herr's reports were prepared

---

131   These elements are indicated in the introduction to the publication of the Bessou Report, a *General Report on the Use of the Cinematograph in Different Branches of Education*, reproduced in the *Revue pédagogique*, First Quarter, 1920.

by calendar year, while the graph uses the academic calendar. A comparison is still possible: the graph shows 22,345 loans for the financial year of 1923–1924 and 25,481 for 1924–1925. This averages to just over 10 loans per film. In the same document, Herr adds:

> "If we take into account that many of these films and series of views are used several times in the same school or school district before being returned, one can easily recognize the constant development of this service."

The success was immense. As with the glass slides, loans were free thanks to the postal service. The museum was the only institution to offer these specialized educational films free of charge. Educational cinema was moving beyond the classroom: teachers organized many extracurricular and after-school sessions for classrooms or reception halls, inviting members of supportive associations as well as parents and friends of the school. Some directors even knew how to develop alternatives to the commercial system in weekly sessions on Thursdays, Saturdays, or Sundays.[132] Even if the pedagogical dimension was not absent from these sessions, the pioneers of educational film were starting to worry about what they saw as a deviation towards spectacle. They were concerned about confusion between educational cinema and entertainment.

Starting in 1925, teachers' complaints proliferated. The reels would wear out from overuse and poorly adapted equipment. Herr was well aware of this issue, which couldn't be solved by buying new films. The public authorities were trying to counteract this problem of wear and tear by adapting the criteria for obtaining a grant for the purchase of distribution equipment. The correspondence between the Minister of Agriculture, whose ministry also possessed a specialized cinematheque, and the Minister of Public Instruction, reproduced in the *Revue pédagogique*, attests to this: "In the presence of this situation, I thought that it would now be possible to significantly reduce the risk of damage to films by making it obligatory from

---

132   Christophe Gauthier, op. cit., p.43.

here on out to use perfectly operating equipment and by only granting subsidies to models approved by our two administrations."[133]

In fact, as of 1921, schools could be reimbursed for all or part of the expenses incurred for projector equipment so long as they submitted a request. But schools were most frequently equipped with devices designed for 9.5mm reels, while the museum only provided 17.5mm films. There would be a commitment to standardization starting in 1927, with the commission of the cinematograph being the reference for technical advice.

Herr would have cinematography play its pioneering role. As early as his note from 1920, he expressed his desire for regionalization, both to relieve the MP but especially to better serve schools outside of Paris and to disseminate new learning methods in the most effective way possible. He would be the architect of this; the enthusiasm aroused by film provoked many initiatives, especially since the MP could not satisfy all requests. Municipalities, general councils, and associations contributed to the establishment of cinema at school through grants and donations. Educational "filmathèques" were emerging in some *départements*, such as in Lyon, where a *filmathèque* of more than 700 films started operating in 1922 under the responsibility of an agent who instructed teachers in how to operate the devices. His activity spanned the Rhône, Isère, Loire, and Ain *départements*. But with the expensive rental of films, this organization had to supplement the subsidies it received from the ministry of public instruction. It was in 1926, with the circular of January 2, that the films service decentralized its loans by organizing departmental and regional repositories under the responsibility of rectors and academy inspectors; now loans were certain to be free and postage allowance guaranteed. In the early 1930s, educational cinema had made its way throughout the territory. Lebrun, who was the assistant director of the MP, estimated that the projectors in circulation due to the MP numbered 10,000.[134]

---

133   Letter of April 14, 1927 from Monsieur le Ministre de l'Agriculture to Monsieur le Ministre de Instruction publique (direction de l'Enseignement primaire) regarding films loaned to schools, in *La Revue pédagogique*, 2nd Quarter 1927.

134   Christophe Gauthier, op. cit., p. 50.

But despite these numerous relay posts, the MP could not even satisfy ten percent of its requests. Its collections were deteriorating more and more and growing obsolete: the museum failed, for example, to adapt to talking cinema. Overall, starting from the middle of the decade, interest in educational cinema slowed significantly. The price of production for educational films and their lack of profitability was aggravated by the incompatibility of different formats and the flammable nature of the medium, which made it unsafe. Attempts to give coherence to the distribution network for educational films was a failure. The pedagogical value of the films even started to be brought into question.[135]

In terms of the MP, Kuntzmann[136] has already wondered if this institution could be considered a mediatheque before its time. It is true that in Herr's time, the museum seemed to have been the ideal place for the cohabitation of the library's traditional functions and new services that were in the process of being invented. The MP promoted the greatest access possible to the documents both on-site and remotely, was very open to new media and even assumed a leading role in this respect, promised all loans free of charge, had a qualified staff, and sought to reach a very broad curricular and after-school "clientele." Herr's diffusionist militancy, driven by his dream of an institute that allowed for democratic access to education, was consistent with this.

Yet the MP did not define itself as a public library. Its patrons and collections were specialized, and even if the cinematograph sessions extended outside school because this is what some instructors wanted, the MP's primary mission was instruction. This is the reason why it benefited from the minister's attention. Moreover, there is no mention of any kind of voluntarism aiming to improve the image of a cultural establishment, even if it were just a matter of "clearing out the cobwebs" and making it more attractive. These problems were historically detailed in the post-war years and even in the 1970s, when a

---

135   Armelle Sentilhes, op. cit., p. 178.

136   Nelly Kuntzmann, op. cit., p. 41.

vast modernization movement changed the model of French libraries. The term "mediatheque" has a connotation of marketing, or in any case of a type of communication, that is not relevant to Herr's time.

Nevertheless, the great vessel that had Herr at the helm for 10 years was really an extraordinary institution that came to approximate the democratic vision that Herr had for it in 1920 and contained the germ of a new model. Before the flagship service of slide and films slipped into inexorable decline, the activities of its directorship had been in some ways the culmination of the MP's project: a pioneering laboratory in the process of inventing a new way of teaching and learning.

Conclusion

At the turn of the century, Lucien Herr was the linchpin of a revolution in the world of ideas and information. On both the production side of ideas as well as on the side of their distribution, he was a representative who was simultaneously exemplary and atypical of the new models being put in place.

First, the production side: Herr was the creator of the new category of intellectual that was taking shape during the period of the Dreyfus Affair. It was in the clash between conservative and militaristic values, on the one hand, and an ideal of justice and truth, on the other, that this social force suddenly emerged on the public stage. This was the thesis of the foundational work of Pascal Ory and Jean-François Sirinelli in their *Histoire des intellectuels en France, de l'Affaire Dreyfus à nos jours* (*History of Intellectuals in France, From the Dreyfus Affair to Today*). Modern intellectuals at the *fin de siècle* were reinventing themselves as they entered the new century. For these two authors, an intellectual was an individual "of culture, a creator and mediator, put in the situation of a politician as a producer and consumer of ideology. This is a status transcended by individual will, turned to a collective use."[137] The Dreyfus Affair was the moment of the intellectual's emergence as a social figure.

---

137   Pascal Ory and Jean-François Sirinelli, *Les Intellectuels, de l'Affaire Dreyfus à nos jours*, Perrin, Paris, 2004, p. 15.

Herr was the exemplary type of this performative definition that has been so historically detailed. He always fought against an obsolete model of elegant erudition in order to defend a useful conception of intelligence oriented towards collective progress. He was the one who drew up the first list of petitioners demanding the review of the captain's trial; who established the army of scholars and Normaliens who defended Dreyfus; who wrote publicly against Barrès to proudly assume, on behalf of all the others, the qualifier of intellectual; who gave this new category the legitimacy of its own existence.

It is striking, however, to see that while Ory and Sirinelli's book may devote many lines to Herr, they remain very allusive. Despite his general recognition as a key character and even as a leader in this emergence, his participation is only briefly mentioned in passing, in sections about someone other than himself. His public appearances and own writings were very limited, and he was less inclined to step into the spotlight to defend an idea than to support it from offstage with all of his strength of force, his consistency, and his legitimacy. The librarian was in some respects an intellectual of the shadows.

At the same time, new models for the dissemination of information were starting to become more flexible, more diverse, better adapted to the democratization of thought and the expansion of literacy; Herr was instrumental on the technical side of processes that made knowledge more accessible to all. It is clear that Herr was at the forefront of the movement and that he attempted to find ways to synthesize all the potentialities for documentation and to generalize new practices. Dissemination in all its forms was at the heart of his practice as a librarian. He was a pioneer and the librarian and bibliographer of his day, even if there is no direct trace that can reconstitute his designs and his possible position on the debates that were transforming the profession at that time.

There was an unresolved tension in Herr between the different social missions he had undertaken: omnipresence on all fronts and a perpetual erasure of traces of his action. This was the counterpart to his activity as a librarian, which required him to become a living encyclopedia in order to accomplish a colossal task: to constitute the ideal library in order to advance collective knowledge.

Paradoxically, Herr had a certain idealism, even though throughout his life he had been a staunch supporter of positivism and rationalism. This idealism manifested as loyalty to great principles that he chose and maintained with unflagging conviction. In the famous letter of 1905 to Andler, for example, he states: "I did what I could to base my personal system of feelings and thoughts on reason." To base on reason—that is, to do nothing in vain, nothing that didn't correspond to a conscious and rational plan; to live out a philosophical destiny, which for him meant destiny in Hegelian terms, with the individual yielding to the advance of the common mind. It's this philosophical interpretation rather than psychological motives that have sometimes been evoked to explain Herr's withdrawal and his renunciation of a brilliant university career; this is the rationale for his career, at once so obscure and so central, as a librarian. Herr was a "complete" intellectual for whom ideas and life were indissociable and who exerted the discipline to ensure that his actions were in keeping with the way of interpreting the world that he found to be the most just. Andler himself explained the astonishing fact that Herr, despite his great knowledge of the issues and reports of international forces, did not foresee the war with Germany. To have better anticipated the war, it would have been necessary not to make ideological Hegelian constructions, to not have such a belief that reason will regulate matters.[138]

It was undoubtedly this intellectual "extremism" undoubtedly this "moral purity" so frequently evoked, that made him modest to the point of neglecting to leave anything behind him, that played a part in cloaking this personality—this character, rather—in legend. Nearly 70 years after the famous letter of 1905, in his final lesson of 1973 at the Collège de France, the Germanist Robert Minder paid tribute to Herr by summarizing the libarian's tragedy

---

138   Charles Andler, op. cit., p. 251.

in striking and theatrical terms: "A devourer of books, a Blue Beard in his own way, flying from one mistress to the next. But do not open the cupboards: the skeletons of unwritten works lie there."[139]

139   Final lecture of May 19, 1973, "Etudes de civilisation germanique: Réflexions et perspectives," Chaire de langues et littératures d'origine germanique, Collège de France, p. 23, cited by Antoinette Blum, op. cit., p. 31.

Sources

Centre d'Histoire de Sciences Po—Archives Lucien Herr

This collection was created thanks to the donation made by Madame Lucien Herr to la Fondation nationale des sciences politiques in 1978. The archives were divided and classified in ten cartons.

The first six (LH1 to LH6) contain Lucien Herr's papers: correspondence, manuscripts, and notes. Three cartons (LH7 to LH10) contain documents assembled by Madame Lucien Herr after her husband's death (1926) until 1979. There are many articles, condolences, correspondence, and papers about ceremonies in Lucien Herr's memory. One carton with images (LH11) completes the collection.

This collection is the richest and most complete available.

- LH1: Life of Lucien Herr
- LH2: Various activities of Lucien Herr
- LH3: Active and passive correspondence (1)
- LH4: Active and passive correspondence (2)
- LH5: Manuscripts, writings, and publications of Lucien Herr (1)
- LH6: Manuscripts, writings, and publications of Lucien Herr (2)
- LH7: Press, speeches, correspondence about the death of Lucien Herr (1)
- LH8: Press, speeches, correspondence about the death of Lucien Herr (2)

- LH9: About some major figures
- LH10: Correspondance of Madame Herr
- LH11: Images

The first carton LH1 contains a dossier entitled "Bibliothèque " (D6).

Archives nationales—Fonds de l'Ecole normale supérieure (Ecole normale supérieure collection)

(series 61 AJ)

Starting in 1971, L'Ecole normale supérieure deposited its archives regarding administration, management, and schooling, which contains directors' papers, student dossiers, and copies of competitive exams, at the Archives Nationales.

Carton 61AJ/157 (General administration—library) corresponds to the period that interests us (1883–1928). This carton contains dossiers on:

- Financial questions (1819–1938)
- Personnel questions, including questions about the succession of Lucien Herr (1926)
- Functioning of the library (regulations)
- Correspondance of Lucien Herr (with the director of the Ecole: 1921, 1924–1926)

The Archives Nationales also keep Herr's personal dossier under call number AJ 16 1137. The consulation of this dossier was subject to special exception. The period for communication prohibited us from being able to consult this document in time.

Library of the Ecole Normale Supérieure

The library of the Ecole normale supérieure preserved a large part of his archives. For Herr's period at the ENS and his direction of the library (1883–1926), it contains:

- the registry for additions to the library of Lettres (1881–1894)
- registry of loans by borrower (1813–1928)
- directories by books borrowed (1868–1928)
- alphabetical and topographic catalogues

Archives nationales—Collection of the Musée Pédagogique (71AJ)

In 1980, the Musée Pédagogique's "historical collections" were divided into two: documents of a more museographic nature were attributed to the Musée de l'Histoire de l'Education, which was transferred to Rouen, while documents of a more archival nature were allocated to the Archives Nationales. This collection covers a period from 1870 to 1968. In addition to the very diverse documents collected by the successive heads of the MP, it includes in particular:

- archives from the Musée Pédagogique (very incomplete)
- works executed upon the request of the minister of public instruction (surveys, statistical charts, scholarly monographs, atlas for primary instruction in 1884)
- Work files of Ferdinand Buisson
- Work files for the preparation of instruction reforms
- A collection of tracts gathered during the events of May 1968

Few of the cartons concern our period. The majority of the documents are surveys that date from the last decades of the nineteenth century or documents concerning the Second World War, or the 1950s. Our attention was focused on dossiers 71 AJ 1 to 6, which contain:

- matters relating to personnel (1882–1927)
- reports, some written by Herr (1909–1927)
- matters related to finances (1904–1952)

Bibliography

Works by Lucien Herr

Collections of texts:

Choix d'écrits. I, Politique, Rieder, Paris, 1932
Choix d'écrits. II, Philosophie, histoire, philologie, Rieder, Paris, 1932

Book reviews:

Revue critique d'histoire et de littérature, from April 1888 to May 1893, under the heading "Bibliography," *Revue universitaire*, from January 1893 to July 1894, heading "Bibliography"

Works about Lucien Herr

Monographs

Andler, Charles: *La vie de Lucien Herr*, François Maspero, Paris, 1977
Blum, Antoinette: *Correspondance entre Charles Andler et Lucien Herr 1891–1926*, Presses de l'Ecole Normale Supérieure, Paris, 1992
Lindenberg, Daniel, and Meyer Pierre-André: *Lucien Herr, le socialisme et son destin*, Calmann Lévy, Paris, 1977

Petitmengin, Pierre: *Lucien Herr et l'Ecole Normale Supérieure*, catalogue de l'exposition présentée à l'ENS du 15 au 30 June 1977, Ecole Normale Supérieure, Paris, 1977

Articles

Andler, Charles: "Lucien Herr," Journal de psychologie normale et pathologique, July 15, 1926, p. 779–87

Fraisse, Simone: "Lucien Herr journaliste 1890–1905," *Le Mouvement social*, July-September 1975, no. 92

Hamel, Maurice: "Lucien Herr et le Musée pédagogique," *L'Alsace française*, 1926, no. 26

Lindenberg, Daniel, "Lucien Herr, une nature dreyfusarde," *Mil neuf cent*, 1993, no.11, p. 31–32

Schoyer, Georges P: "Lucien Herr, Librarian and Socialist," The Journal of Library History (1974–1987), 1975

Verley, Etienne, "Lucien Herr et le positivisme," Romantisme, 1978, no.21–22, p. 219–32

Political and social history

Monographs

Blum, Léon: *Mes souvenirs sur l'Affaire*, Gallimard, Paris, 1935

Bourgin, Hubert: *De Jaurès à Léon Blum, l'Ecole normale et la politique*, Fayard, Paris, 1938

Charle, Christophe, and Verger, Jacques: *Histoire des universités*, PUF, Paris, 2007

Merle, Pierre: *Histoire de la démocratisation de l'enseignement*, PUF, Paris 2009

Ory, Pascal and Sirenelli, Jean-François: *Les Intellectuels en France, de l'Affaire Dreyfus* à *nos jours*, Armand Colin, Paris, 1992

Prost, Antoine: *Histoire de l'enseignement en France*, 1800–1967, Colin, Paris, 1970

Winock, Michel: *Le siècle des intellectuels*, Seuil, Paris, 1992

Articles

John Smith, Robert, "L'atmosphère politique à l'ENS à la fin du 19ème
   siècle," *Revue d'histoire*

moderne et contemporaine, April June 1973, no.20.

Winock, Michel, *Mélanges d'histoire sociale offerts à Jean Maitron*,
   Editions ouvrières, 1976

History of information and libraries

Monographs

Bertrand, Anne-Marie: *Les bibliothèques*, La Découverte, Paris, 2007

Centre National de la Documentation pédagogique: *Le Musée
   pédagogique d'hier à aujourd'hui 1879–1979*, INRP, Paris, 1979

Fayet-Scribe, Sylvie, *Histoire de la documentation en France, Culture,
   science et technologie de l'information 1895–1937*, CNRS, Paris, 2000

Articles

Delmas, Bruno: "Une fonction nouvelle: genèse et développement des
   centres de documentation," in Martine Poulain (dir.), Histoire des
   bibliothèques françaises, Vol 4: Les bibliothèques au 20ème siècle
   1914–1990, Cercle de la Librairie, Paris, 2009

Hebrard, Jean: "Les bibliothèques scolaires: l'impossible pari des
   bibliothèques circulantes," in Dominique VARRY (dir.): *Histoire des
   bibliothèques françaises*, Vol 3, *Les bibliothèques de la Révolution et du
   19ème siècle*, Paris, Cercle de la Librairie, 2009

Sentilhes, Armelle: "L'audio-visuel au service de l'enseignement:
   projections lumineuses et cinéma scolaire, 1880–1940," *La Gazette
   des Archives*, 2ème trimestre 1996, no. 173

Vidal de la Bache, Paul, "La Bibliothèque de l'Ecole," Le centenaire de
   l'ENS 1795–1895, Ecole Normale Supérieure, Paris, 1895, p. 447–53

Student Works

Gauthier, Christophe: *A l'école de la mémoire, La constitution d'un réseau de cinémathèques en milieu scolaire 1899- 1928*, Mémoire DCB, ENSSIB, 1997

Kuntzmann, Nelly: *Des images pour le dire, des mots pour le voir. Prémisses de la culture audiovisuelle,* éducation *et bibliothèque, 1895–1940*, Mémoire DCB, ENSSIB, 1997

Webography

Resource dossiers on the history of education, available on the INRP site "Les bibliothèques en France": http://www.inrp.fr/vst/Dossiers/Histoire/Bibliotheques/bib_france.htm

"Les manuels scolaires à l'INRP ": http://www.inrp.fr/vst/Dossiers/Histoire/manuels.htm

Table of Appendices

Appendix 1

Lucien Herr's letter of application for the position of librarian at the Ecole (December 11, 1887)

Paris, Wednesday December 11, 1887

Monsieur le Directeur,

I am, unfortunately, extraordinarily shy. You asked me yesterday, with your infinite benevolence, about my desires and my dreams. My visit had no other purpose than to tell you, and I did not tell you.

You already know. I wrote to you about it more than six months ago. The library at the Ecole represents all of my dreams and my ambitions. While I made the first advances as a candidate, in a letter dated from Germany, I have not obtained any answer from you on this point. I did not dare insist. It took Monsieur Boutroux, whom I informed of my ambitions, to encourage me to broach the matter with you again.

This is the only thing I want, and it's what I've dreamed of and have wanted for years. Please take my request into consideration with all the kindness you have constantly shown me. I tell you in all simplicity that you would cause me infinite sorrow in countering my request with a categorical refusal. If there is no hope for the near future, leave it to me for later. I will wait, very patiently. I may have some titles. Monsieur Rébelliau can tell you that I'm very familiar with the library, and that I have used it a lot. I don't view the librarian position as temporary, but rather full-time and permanent, at least many years, and I would agree in advance to undertake the immense task of reorganizing the catalog—something that I know is very necessary. My entire dedication is, or would be, a foregone conclusion.

Do you require other titles than I might have? If you absolutely want my theses to be made for the day when the vacancy is declared, I accept the appointment ahead of time. Are there other conditions you consider necessary? I commit in advance: I am prepared to do anything.

You can tell, Monsieur Director, how earnestly I desire this. You would not believe the value I ascribe to it. I've lived with this hope for months, for years. I ask you, in the name of all your kindness towards me, not to take it away from me. I ask you to take my attempts into consideration and to think of my very sincere intentions, as you well know, of serious work. I recommend myself to you with confidence; but you can not imagine the state of anxiety I am in as I await your answer.

With my sincerest respect and devotion.

Signed: Lucien Herr

11, rue du Val de Grâce

Appendix 2

Paris, November 22, 1890

Monsieur le Directeur,

I had the honor of informing you, at the end of the first quarter of this year, of my concerns arising from the comparison of credits issued for our library and figures for foreseeable expenses, some of which were engaged previously, and others that are either indispensable or very useful. I then explained to you that on the one hand, the credit regularly attributed to the library being notoriously insufficient, and on the other hand, the remainder of the general budget for the Ecole being drawn in a rapidly descending progression that no longer allows for any illusions of possible recovery, it became impossible to cope with an increasing deficit other than by reducing purchases, which would amount to suicide; I also added that it would be difficult to find someone who would let a unique library like ours crumble in his hands.

You have received these desperate grievances with kindness, and you have asked me to budget expenses to the point of miserliness for the year. I pushed it to the limit, showing no weakness; I am battling against recriminations and insults, which, as you know, have not been in short supply. I submit to you today the budgetary results of this year of deprivation.

The library's annual expenditures in the last ten years have been constantly higher than 12,000, and most often 13,000 francs. This does not include exceptional years, where we could go up to 16,638.65 francs or 15,501.50 francs. I'm keeping to the average years. When the balances started to decline, the regular budget was raised from 5,600 to 8,000 francs. The total amount of the expenditures deemed necessary could thus remain the same.

The financial year of 1888 gave me identical results. The remainders made it possible to deal with expenses slightly higher than 12,000 francs. This first financial year and data from previous years delineated the limits that I could consider fixed. The financial year of 1889 disappointed my expectations: the total figure for expenditure was 12,473.45; the sum of the resources available turned out to be only 10,823.35. The deficit of 1650.10 had to be carried forward to the 1890 financial year, which was thus seriously threatened.

I was warned that the sum of the remaining balances, which had diminished so much last year, would have to undergo renewed reduction this year, bringing it close to zero. Expenses have been constrained beyond all acceptable restrictions.

Here is the proof. The sum of the expenses for the year, including the approximate evaluation that would result, from now until December 31, for renewing su[b]scriptions and essential purchases, will be about 9,500 francs; when adding the deficit of 1,650 francs from last year, there is a total charge of 11,150 francs.

To deal with this, the library has its ordinary credit of 8,000 francs. If the balance is zero, we will find ourselves with a deficit of 3,150 francs, which will heavily burden the 1891 financial year. The following detail will make it clear that it was impossible to further restrict expenses. Bookbinding is included in this year's expenditure for a total of about 2,500 francs. The average expenditure from previous years for bookbinding costs was close to 3,900 francs. The reduction was 1,400 francs. It was impossible to go further without compromising the life of the books, at least without exposing them to wear, making usage impossible or very difficult.

Fees for periodical subscriptions amount to more than 3,000 francs. In this regard, any serious economizing is impossible. We keep strictly to periodicals that are informational and work instruments that are entirely necessary. By no stretch of the imagination have we caused an excessive increase in the number of journals that are in some way useful. We do not receive a single periodical that is a luxury.

About 2,500 francs are attributable to the series of works to which we have subscribed. For such series, we possess the first volume and it is impossible to interrupt the purchase without breaking our commitments and leading to disorganization of the library. Any reduction in this regard therefore seems impossible.

There remain approximately 1,500 francs for the purchase of new works. The sum is laughable, and it was only possible to keep within the limits of this excessively reduced amount by deliberately abandoning the possibility of enriching the library with recently published works that would sustain its status and allow it to remain the work instrument of the first order it has been so far. We can agree to such extremes for one year, as an experiment; a few years of this regimen would be the end of us.

The situation is thus compromised to the point of desparation. First, the economizing measures have been pushed beyond the limits of the possible, and this regimen, if continued for a few years, would result in the rapid ruin of our library.

Secondly, this regimen presents an extreme that cannot be exceeded, supposing there were a desire to adhere to it for a few years, and would itself be insufficient, since it entails a higher annual expenditure of 1,500 francs more than the regular credits, the only ones on which we can now rely. Finally, supposing that the existence of the library were ensured for the years to come, we are now smothered by the deficit of more than 3,000 francs which awaits us on December 31, and that we will never succeed in liquidating, unless somebody comes to our aid.

Allow me, Monsieur Directeur, to draw from this lamentable picture the practical consequences that could be our salvation. On the one hand, I do not believe it possible, in the current state of literary and scientific production, to maintain a contemporary library without a guaranteed credit of at least 12,000 francs (less than the average of expenditures over the last ten years). On the other hand, I only see a cure to the difficulties of our present situation in an extraordinary credit which allow us to liquidate our liabilities.

Yours respectfully and faithfully,

Signed: Lucien Herr.

Appendix 3

Monsieur le Directeur,

The library of the Ecole owes the sum of 19,500 francs as of October 1st, with the amount broken down as follows:

- Klincksieck: 14,000 francs
- Other bookstores: 4,500
- Bookbinders: 1,000

Between now and December 31, it will be necessary to anticipate, as new expenses incurred in advance or as necessary expenses (series of works, renewals of subscriptions to periodicals, binding) about 2,500 francs, which will be broken down roughly as follows:

- Kincksieck: 1,000 francs
- Other booksellers: 1,000
- Binding: 500

As of 31 December, the total debt will therefore amount to approximately 22,000 francs. I think that, to be fair, it will be necesary to deduct from this debt about 1,000 francs, which represents subscriptions to periodicals that expire in the second half of the year 1902, and so are in truth an advance made on the budget for 1903, and needing, according to the usual practice, to be entered in the account for the 1903 budget.

The exact debt would therefore be about 21,000 francs.

To deal with this debt, the resources are as follows:

- 3,437.80 francs remaining for the regular credit of 8,190 (of which 4,572.20 have been paid)
- The extraordinary credit granted each year to the library, which has been 5,000 francs in previous years, and 6,000 francs at the end of 1901. Total assets will therefore be, depending on whether the extraordinary credit is 6,000 or 5,000 francs, 8,500 or 9,500 francs. Thus, at the end of the year 1902, the library will have a deficit of 11,500 or 12,500 francs, depending on whether the extraordinary credit granted will be 6,000 or 5,000 francs.

I ask you, Monsieur le Directeur, to listen to the explanations that I request to present to you as succinctly as possible.

Exceeding credits is, in the matter of buying books, a practice that is standard because it is unavoidable, and it is not possible to make rigorously precise predictions about expenditures for such an uncertain matter. It was impossible, for example, to predict that over the last few months three expensive volumes of the Greek and Latin corpus, and several expensive volumes of *Monuments Germanica Historica*, would be published. It is impossible to predict the exact date when the very costly volumes on the fauna of the Gulf of Naples, or on the Antichi Monuments, will appear. At the beginning of this year, I could not anticipate that we would subscribe to ten or twelve volumes that supplement the Encyclopedia Britannica, and that it would be necessary to subscribe in advance, and to pay in advance a sum of £13 for volumes of which the last will not be published until 1903, so as to avoid having to pay near double once the subscription period has come to a close. These uncertainties challenge any predictability. These are reasons of this kind, with an extraordinary accumulation of series of works, to explain why supplies from Klincksieck during the first eight months of the year totaled nearly 5,000 francs, whereas since late 1901 I have strictly enforced the rule that we only take from Klincksieck series of works that were subscribed to and accepted in advance, renewals of subscriptions to periodicals, and to reduce the new purchases as such to nothing. Exceeding credits was, for yet another reason, what was normal at the time that I was entrusted with the library. You will remember that at the time it had resources for which the total varied from year to year, and which consisted of ordinary credit, plus the Ecole's budgetary surpluses for the rest.

These resources, which had increased to 16,000 francs, would oscillate between 13,000 and 15,000. From the first years of my entry into service, I pointed out the difficulty that there was in organizing the purchases in a careful and precise manner, while there remained such uncertainty regarding the total for the annual budgets. All in all, caution may have been the worst method, since it led to suddenly finding ourselves with a surplus that we had to use as quickly as possible for general purchases, while the methodical use of that same sum over the entire year was a precious resource. By acting prudently, we were thus brought through our prudence to expect the maximum surplus, and to use it in confidence, in the best interests of the library–at the risk of being faced, at the end of the year, with a total credit that was less than anticipated.

As budget surpluses dwindled I signaled the very great difficulty that had to be faced, with a budget in worrying decline, with charges that were increasing incessantly. In a very detailed report, I insisted first on the urgent need, so as to avoid miscalculations, of a certain budget that was not susceptible to unforeseen reductions,–and on the near-impossibility of surviving, with fewer regular resources, on fewer than 14 or 15,000 francs, with the increase in normal expenses and extraordinary expenses that were incumbent upon the library. The increase in regular charges was the normal growth in the useful and increasingly necessary production in the sciences as well as in history and literature; but the heavy and worrying charges, the extraordinary charges, had other causes that I can only briefly recall, because to focus on them would be to tell the whole history of the Ecole's past fifteen years. I only want to recall the creations and innovations that made the constitution or the rapid, almost immediate growth of categories of books which scarcely existed, or were very badly represented, so essential. First, there were the arrangements at the Ecole for the instruction and study of natural sciences, which burdened the budget with the need to make a considerable number of expensive subscriptions. It was then the creation of the living language sections, which, quite deprived of work instruments at the outset, had to be equipped very quickly, taking advantage of opportunities to fill gaps that were too severe by immediately constituting the first indispensable stock of classic texts and course books, etc. There was then the very rapid development of contemporary history studies, which necessitated the speedy acquisition of a fairly large number of books that were completely missing from the library. There was the continuous development of geographic studies, which required the expensive enrichment of a section that was very poorly represented when I was called to the library. We mustn't forget an incident that had rather difficult consequences for the library, the departure of Monsieur Chuquet. When he left, he retracted the free usage of periodicals, the annual subscription price for which was at least a thousand francs. More than half were of considerable importance and were now being charged to our budget. I did not blindly yield to requests from teachers or students, but I had to give in to obvious emergencies and undeniably fair demands, and these new charges accumulated, adding to the burden of normal expenses. The inevitable consequence was that credits were exceeded.

This was, for some sections, a kind of first-time fee, and it was clearly unfair to impute it to the year they were incurred; it would be fair, however, to liquidate such a fee in a few years through annuities. I knew that as soon as the burdensome, necessary sacrifices were made, it would be easier to restrict purchases, to limit them strictly, and to gradually amortize the debt. In reality, the burden on the library was greater two years ago than it is today, with spending for the last two years remaining below the annual credits, and I am sure that in three or four years the current debt could be easily eradicated if the extraordinary allowances were to remain equal to what they were for the year 1901.

I am certain I did not act lightly or carelessly. While making sure that this excellent and precious library did not fall to pieces in my hands, I had to give in to the onerous and imperious demands of the new orders of studies and work undertaken at the Ecole, and I consciously accepted the responsibility of a financial burden that was heavy but also temporary, and that a few years would suffice to ease. I know, and I knew it would have been more prudent on my part to have taken no initiative, to have made the purchases required by the faculty within the limits of the budgetary resources, and stopped there. If I proceeded otherwise, it was deliberately, out of the passionate dedication to the work that has been entrusted to me. For fifteen years, the library has been my daily concern. My only thought every day was to embellish and enrich the beautiful instrument I had in my hands. I am aware that I have done my best. I did not proceed as a bibliophile or a maniacal collector, but rather took every care so that for all the works, today more differentiated and more varied than ever, that are undertaken at the Ecole, the primary, the best of the instruments needed were there. I knew it would always be impossible to complete a special scholarly work with our resources alone, but I thought it should be possible to undertake and outline any work using our resources.

I have done what I could to put myself in a position to assess the necessary work instruments. I would not say that none of my acquisitions are questionable, but I can say that there is not a single one that I made lightly, without examination, without study, without reflection. The unanimous esteem for our library serves as a guarantee that the efforts have not been in vain. I considered this library as a living organism that needed to be strengthened and developed methodically. I always thought it had to guide, enlighten, and solicit work, and not merely follow it. New directions of pupils' work, the expansion of their scholarly curiosity, the works of history, especially contemporary history, of philosophy, geography, and sociology, which are now the pride of the Ecole –it would have been impossible to undertake all these works even with the resources that our library had fifteen years ago, and I find in them an acknowledgment and reward for my efforts.

I would have liked to say less hurriedly, less confusedly, less feebly, all these things that I know to be true, and the expression of which remains, in spite of myself, incomplete and imperfect. I regret not having done better, and I regret having been dominated by an emotion that I do not master—and please accept, Monsieur Director, the expression of my highest devotion.

Signed: Lucien Herr

Appendix 4

Letter From Lucien Herr To Charles Andler (September 25, 1905)

(...)

It is absolutely necessary that you make available to a general public this tremendous work of guidance and understanding that is not made just for your students ... This is what distresses me the most, in my *vie manquée*. I know the services that I have provided, and I do not need to be comforted; but I also know everything that I have really learned, known, and understood—at least in my own way—of things, and how absurd it is that the community cannot take advantage of these long years of work, and that others will have to do them again. What would my life be like, if I were to reorganize it—and would it leave me the leisure and the desire to get a hold of the things I have known, one by one, and push them further and set them down, and would I be able to extract something that is communicable and that is worth being communicated? I do not know, and I doubt it. (...)

For each subject, big or small, that I've I touched, each time I've seen myself led to push my study as far as possible, out of an irresistible need and voracious curiosity, to not content myself with preconceptions, to get the documents back in my hands and do the critical work again. I have, on the way, found quite a few points (particularly in patristics, religious history, in Celtic studies), things that have since been discovered by others, for my own pleasure; but I never cared much. I had various specialties, but I was never an expert, and I always considered myself satisfied when I understood (or believed I understood) the whole or the detail that had given me pause or seduced me (...)

You know all this as well as I do. This is true even of the two big subjects that I dreamed of devoting my life to, twenty years ago—the history of Hegelianism and the history of Platonism. What will I find when I really stir all the ashes that were extinguished so long ago and forgotten? Without a doubt, very little.–And then, my mind and my heart are gone, I am no longer interested in things that are purely speculative. I am only capable of passionate interest in what leads to practice, to intellectual and social development.

Adieu, kiss the little ones. I send to you, for your wife and for yourself, all my old faithful friendship.

Lucien Herr."

Index